LONGING
for
LOVE

MICHAEL FROST

LONGING

for

LOVE

GENDER, SEXUALITY AND
OUR EXPERIENCE OF GOD

AN ALBATROSS BOOK

© Michael Frost, 1996

Published in Australia and New Zealand by
Albatross Books Pty Ltd
PO Box 320, Sutherland
NSW 2232, Australia
in the United States of America by
Albatross Books Pty Ltd
PO Box 131, Claremont
CA 91711, USA
and in the United Kingdom by
Lion Publishing plc
Peter's Way, Sandy Lane West
Oxford OX4 5HG, England

First edition 1996

National Library of Australia
Cataloguing-in-Publication data

Frost, Michael
Longing for Love

ISBN 0 7324 1059 2

1. Sex — Religious aspects — Christianity. 2. Masculinity of God.
3. Femininity of God. 4. God — Love. I. Title.

231.7

Cover photograph: Graham Horner
Printed and bound in Australia by Griffin Paperbacks, Netley, SA

CONTENTS

To my dearest friend and wife,
Carolyn

INTRODUCTION

IN 1913, THE AMERICAN POET, ROBERT FROST, published his whimsical poem 'Mending Wall' in a book called *North of Boston*, in which he posed an important philosophical question about walls. The question is never answered in the poem; instead we, the readers, happen upon two neighbours involved in the ancient and traditional business of maintaining the stone wall that divides their farms:

> . . .*The gaps I mean,*
> *No-one has seen them made or heard them made,*
> *But at spring mending-time we find them there.*
> *I let my neighbour know beyond the hill;*
> *And on a day we meet to talk the line*
> *And set the walls between us as we go.*[1]

Frost points out that this is a silly ritual. It's not as if they run sheep or cattle that may stray into the neighbour's propety. Pine trees and apple orchards hardly need to be separated. They just rebuild the wall because. . . well, *because*! That's the game they share together. There's nothing to wall in or out, just a broken wall to mend, just fallen stones to replace:

> *We wear our fingers rough with handling them.*
> *Oh, just another kind of outdoor game,*
> *One on a side. It comes to little more:*
> *There where it is we do not need the wall:*
> *He is all pine and I am apple orchard.*
> *My apple trees will never get across*
> *And eat the cones under his pines, I tell him.*
> *He only says, 'Good fences make good neighbours.'* [2]

Such a neatly expressed pirce of New England wisdom seems to stand on its own merit: good fences make good neighbours. But Frost's narrator questions such wisdom: 'Why do they make good neighbours?' And why indeed! 'Mending Wall' never answers such a query. It leaves us wondering about stone walls and neighbourliness. Why do good fences make good neighbours?

Perhaps it's because good fences, clear boundaries, are the common ground between those who live close by each other. Maybe we are better friends when we know what it is that separates us, makes us different. Could it be that pine trees and apple trees are better discerned as groves and orchards when separated by a stone wall?

The understated wisdom of Robert Frost (no relation, mind you) is that we could be better friends if we met more often at the stone wall and engaged in the apparently silly, and yet necessary, ritual of reaffirming our differences as neighbours. In the midst of the current discussion regarding gender relations, perhaps a celebration of the stone wall between men and women would not be such a bad thing.

Men and women *are* different. So plain a statement seems unnecessary and yet in all the hullabaloo about equality between the sexes we've almost forgotten that two can be equal without being the same. When we look at the differences between masculinity and femininity, we become overwhelmed by the question as to which is superior. We ask, 'If men and women are so different, who's on top?' For centuries, men have assumed they were on top. Now men feel strangely uncomfortable with the fact that women may, in fact, be superior, after all. A trip to the stone wall that marks us off from each other might remind us that our differences are to be celebrated and embraced, rather than set in competition with each other.

Another whimsical, though more contemporary, American writer is Garrison Keillor. In one of the charming stories in his collection of tales about masculinity, *The Book of Guys*, he satirises the growing fear among men that the world now sees women as superior to them:

> *Years ago, manhood was an opportunity for achievement, and now it is a problem to be overcome. . . They are trying to be Mr OK All-Rite, the man who can bake a cherry pie, go play baseball, come home, make melon balls and whip up a great soufflé, converse easily about intimate matters, participate in recreational weeping, laugh, hug, be vulnerable, be passionate in a skilful way, and the next day go off and lift them bales into that barge and tote it. A guy who women consider acceptable.*[3]

As he points out in just about every one of his twenty-one stories, men have lost their means of understanding masculinity. The boundaries have been blurred. The stone wall needs mending and men are afraid in these politically correct days to do so. But such is the call. We need to reaffirm the differences in order to be better neighbours. Because, as Keillor says, 'Being all right is a dismal way to spend your life, and guys are not equipped for it anyway. We are lovers and artists and adventurers, meant to be noble, free-ranging and foolish, like dogs, not competing for a stamp of approval, *Friend of Womanhood.*'[4]

You may or may not agree with his celebration of manhood. It doesn't matter at this point. His affirmation about the nature of masculinity is his attempt at wandering down to the stone wall to rebuild it. Those men and women who imagine quality equals sameness are content to leave the fence in disarray, refusing to believe that good, sturdy fences make good, solid neighbours. When we end up grading ourselves on some scale of sameness, we sacrifice neighbourliness. Garrison Keillor goes on: 'Now women watch us and monitor our conversations for signs of bad attitude, they grade us daily, and boys, we are in the wrong class. Men can never be feminists. Millions have tried and nobody did better than a C+.'[5]

While ever we refuse to acknowledge gender differences, we're trying to cross-fertilise pine trees and apple orchards, something Robert Frost thought ludicrous. This is not to suggest that men and women don't have something to learn from each other. Teasing out the best opposite sex traits from within is perfectly healthy. But to do so is not to create some third strain, a new androgynous being. Rather, it's about going to the stone wall and celebrating our differences while still being open to learn a thing or two from our neighbour's strengths.

If men and women are to be neighbours, we need to mend some walls. And for that matter, if people and God are to be friends, we need some walls, also. Not walls that create division and strife, but healthy appreciations of boundaries and limits. In Frost's poem, the narrator is unconvinced of the need for walls, but his neighbour finds security in the wisdom of his forefathers. Today, many voices call us to disregard the differences between men and women and between God and humankind. But men are not women, and humans cannot be God. This book will be an attempt to mend some badly damaged walls, to rebuild some boundaries, so that we can better be ourselves and not something other think we should be.

Garrison Keillor, with his tongue firmly in his cheek, demonstrates how awkward and pathetic is the attempt to please our neighbours without the benefit of good fences:

> *Guys know that we should free ourselves from women stake out our own turf and stop trying to be so wonderful to them. Let women deal with their own lives and solve their own problems. Stop feeling guilty as if we could make it up to them.*[6]

Later on he reports:

> *Women can rule the world, fine, but we need them to love us again, or else it's no good.*

> 'Why is it important to you to be as wonderful as you
> are?' a woman asked me one night a I lay sobbing into a
> pillow, having made a cherry pie that tasted like some
> sparrows had been baked into it. 'Why can't you just be
> yourself?' [7]

I am convinced that if we were all more able to be
ourselves and let others be themselves and let God be
himself, we'd be far better off. This book will explore
the walls we rightly need to build between masculinity
and femininity, between sexuality and genitality, between God and humankind, between grace and effort,
between love and making love.

But as much as we need to rebuild the lines of
distinction between ourselves and God, we will also need
to tear some phoney walls down, particularly the walls
we've built to fence God in. If we're to be good
neighbours to God, we need to abandon some unhelpful
assumptions along the way. One of those assumptions
has to do with the gender perceptions we foist onto
God. God is not a sexual being, but we have broken
down the fences that separate him from us and try to
make God in our own image.

For example, a great deal of Christian thinking and
theology has been based on the very fundamental principle that God is masculine and that the human soul is
feminine. I can't overestimate how great an impact this
single assumption has had on the church and the way it
has interacted with our world.

As a result, much of the way in which we understand God and the various metaphors we use to describe
him are almost exclusively male — and an old-fashioned,

Eisenhower kind of 1950s male at that. On the other hand, our language for describing our spirituality has been very feminine. And again, this has been language that reflects the pre-sexual revolution female — submissive, weak and inferior.

My concern has been that we have allowed the timeless realities of God and human spirituality to become time-locked in a bygone era when to be masculine was to be tough, strong and dependable and to be feminine was to be sweet, pretty and dependent. God has been caricatured as the ultimate Eisenhower man who feels no pain, who solves every problem, who wins every battle. And the human brain has been described as a scatterbrained, helpless, impulsive young girl.

Hopefully, we no longer accept these kinds of stereotypes when looking at gender issues. Over the past thirty years, the traditional Western ideas about the proper roles of men and women have broken down, with little consensus in sight as to what should replace them.

While I accept that there is much work still to be done in the area of gender justice, I still believe this is, in fact, an exciting time with great possibilities. A slate is being wiped clean. In what ways will the Christian experience contribute to what will be written there? For there is no question that the Christian experience underpins much of our cultural presuppositions. And yet, sadly, Christian theology seems to be still caught up with the sexual language as expressed by the generation that gave us *I Love Lucy* and *Father Knows Best*. They are inadequate metaphors for the experience of God.

What I have attempted to do in this book is to look at the ancient wisdom concerning God as collected in the Bible and to free the variety of metaphors, both masculine and feminine, that are contained there. I trust that what we will find is an experience of God that crosses gender barriers with ease, that shatters our preconceptions and that releases us from demanding too much from God or too little from ourselves.

This may seem a provocative statement to some, but I genuinely believe that the outdated gender stereotypes we foist onto God and the human soul have contributed to so many people's disappointment with the Christian faith. The church has presented a vision of God not unlike Superman — another 1950s masculine icon — the man of steel for whom no challenge is too great. And yet, for many of us, God has not revealed himself in the classic competent, controlling, male way. We have been disappointed in him when he hasn't come through for us in the way we might have expected.

And, of course, neither have we sensed that our own spirituality is the dainty flower of femininity as presented by the church. We have become more feisty, more pragmatic about wanting a liberating experience of a robust and confident spirituality that takes seriously our sexuality and our gender.

Surely, it's time to rediscover the complexity of our spirituality and sexuality and the depth of the character of God as detailed in the Bible, so that we might be free to embrace a far richer, less optimistic, more realistic faith that helps us track our way through this chaotic and haphazard world.

Good fences make good neighbours — and we desperately need some fences to reinforce in our minds what makes God God and humans humans.

I must also say that this would be a very different and vastly inferior book were it not for the contributions of the following people. I owe them all a great debt of gratitude.

My wife Carolyn has been a great source of nurture and support. She has read every draft and, while I cannot point out any specific page, paragraph or phrase that she has contributed directly, her feminist theology and her desire for justice in gender relations permeate the whole project.

Merilyn Correy and Cath Taylor read the penultimate draft and were both brutally frank in making many helpful suggestions for improvements. Their feminine perspectives were very confronting for a married male like myself. Their input has been invaluable and I thank them deeply. Also, Karl Faase is a good mate who helped me focus the general direction of this book in a different way to that which I had originally envisaged. By so doing, he has saved me much embarrassment.

As with my first book, *Jesus the Fool*, my editor, Ken Goodlet from Albatross, has been nothing short of marvellous in creating another silk purse out of a sow's ear. And I am also indebted to John Waterhouse at Albatross for his great support.

While most of this book has been written at Morling College in Sydney, using their time and resources and enjoying their companionship and encouragement, some of it has been written 'on the road', so to speak. There are sections I can point to and know that I wrote on a laptop in Perth, New York or North Carolina, on scraps of paper in Indonesia, Singapore and Newcastle, at retreats at Galston or conferences in Melbourne, or at Burleigh College in Adelaide.

And so to those many people who support my work and nurture my involvement in teaching and speaking around Australia and beyond, I thank you also from the bottom of my heart.

Michael Frost
Balgowlah, NSW
Australia

1

SEXUALITY AND GOD

Where our deepest yearnings for love come from

> *Sex is like going to the supermarket: lots of pushing and shoving and not much to show for it.*
>
> Shirley Valentine
>
> *Lord, grant me chastity. . . but not yet!*
>
> St Augustine

IT'S AN INTERESTING PHENOMENON that we humans seem destined to *yearn!* Built into the very fabric of our psyches or our genes, we can't help hungering after more than is our current experience. Our yearning for the ultimate experience appears to dog us at every juncture. I think it's one of the distinguishing features of the human race: the yearning *for more!*

Why do you think it is that, when we enter a bookshop, we hold deep within us the hope that this time we just might stumble upon the ultimate book, the one that will say it all and answer every question we have about life, the universe and everything? When we take a table at our favourite restaurant, why do we secretly yearn for the perfect meal, the banquet to end all banquets, the feast that will never be forgotten?

Isn't every trip to the mailbox an expression of hope that we will return with *that* letter, the one that will truly 'make our day'? Even when all the evidence from a hundred previous trips suggests there will be nothing there but bills and junk mail, we still yearn for that ultimate and surprising discovery.

Surely, every December brings with it the dream that this will be the unforgettable Christmas, the one where everything works out perfectly. Doesn't every anniversary and vacation throw up the same promise? Isn't every date, every sporting contest, every computer game, every wave, every throw of the dice pregnant with the same promise? It's the promise of the possibility of the ultimate experience.

Our yearning for the ultimate is nowhere more evident than in the expression of a couple of our most basic experiences: our sexuality and our spirituality. When we begin to examine human sexuality closely, we see human yearning at its most raw. Our sexuality is about more than our desire to be physically gratified — though it certainly holds that promise. It is the promise of an ultimate reality. It is the yearning for ultimate connections, for meaning, for love, for togetherness, for companionship, for forgiveness and for life beyond.

A terrific band from Melbourne called 'Things of Stone And Wood' released their first album in 1993 called 'The Yearning'. The title track clearly expresses what I'm saying:

It's in the hand that heals,
It's in the hand that blesses,
It's in the hand that kills,
It's in the hand that seeks redemption,
By gently stroking the bruises of its fury's crimes.
This is the search for a god
This is the horror of mortality
This is the shadow of death tormenting me.
This is the yearning for more,
The yearning for more than this,
I yearn.

✠ All human experience points us towards God

I believe that the source of all ultimate reality is in the mind of God and so, when we look at such deep, personal human realities as sexuality, we are on a course to the divine.

This could be said of all human experiences of a deeply personal nature — they draw us towards God. They offer us hints at what the Ultimate Reality looks like. When we examine the human yearnings for justice, love and nourishment, we are moving in the direction of God himself.

The great Christian thinker, C.S. Lewis, said something very similar to this in a remarkable sermon called 'The Weight of Glory' that he preached at England's Oxford University in 1941. He believed all human hunger, all our appetites, are reminders of the ultimate hunger for the divine. Our sexual appetite is no different. When we explore human sexuality, we are dealing with human spirituality. And human spirituality, I believe, derives from the one Spirit — from God.

When we seek to gratify ourselves sexually, we are also, perhaps unknowingly, yearning to make basic, core spiritual connections. Since sex is about my body, my masculinity, my psyche, my quest for love, acceptance and security, my want for pleasure, power and meaning, then it deals with profound spiritual realities. When many people, particularly through the sexual revolution of the 'sixties and 'seventies, imagined that sexual intercourse was a purely physiological function, like eating or sleeping, they were wrong. In fact, it's wrong to assume eating and sleeping are *only* physiological functions. Since we are not made up of bodies, psyches and spirits as mutually exclusive compartments of humanness, bodily functions are normally interconnected with spiritual and emotional ones. We *are* body/psyche/spirit: a single reality with three facets.

Eating, for example, is about more than simply meeting the physiological need for sustenance and nourishment. If it was, why would so many people feel self-conscious about eating alone in a restaurant? Why do those who live alone feel their aloneness most clearly at meal times? It's because eating is also about community, celebration and solidarity with others. At the very least, it's about sharing. Eating alone will certainly sustain your body, but it's never as good as eating with others. There is clearly a spiritual component to the consumption of food.

Likewise with sleeping. For a start, few of us like to sleep alone, just as few people enjoy eating alone. But there's more to it. Sleeping and dreaming put us in touch with deeper realities than those within our consciousness. How does one explain our capacity to dream unless we see it as an opportunity for the spiritual to invade the temporal in the context of a simple physiological need like rest or relaxation? We honestly cannot separate out physiological and spiritual functions as though they were mutually exclusive.

So, as C.S. Lewis pointed out, human desire, the deep longing for something that will satisfy us physically, calls us beyond finite objects and finite persons. As much as we seek satisfaction in books or music, food or sleep, sex or sport, we seek spiritual satisfaction. And I also agree with Lewis that such fulfilment comes only in God himself. In 1941, he said:

> *For they [physical pleasures] are not the thing itself; they are only the scent of a flower we have not found, the echo of a tune we have not heard, news from a country we have not visited.*[1]

Like news from a far-off land, like the whiff of an unseen flower, like echoes of an unheard tune, so is our yearning for the ultimate. It is our psycho-spiritual desire for connection with the source of all truth, with God himself.

Human sexuality is likewise. It is a beautiful and mystical experience that sends us news from a country we have not visited. It echoes the tune of another reality — spiritual reality. An honest appraisal of our sexuality will open doors, I believe, on that other country — the place where God dwells. Richard Holloway, Bishop of Edinburgh, says, in his book *Anger, Sex, Doubt and Death*:

Sexuality is a figure or symbol of our ultimate destiny with God, because it is a search for the other. We feel that it is not good for us to be alone. We feel mysteriously incomplete, so all our life is a searching for a remembered unity we have never yet known. Sexuality is one of the modes of our search; it is both a symptom of our incompleteness and a sign of our fulfilment. For the Christian, therefore, there are two ingredients in sexual experience. One is clearly participation in the joy of God.[2]

Lewis went so far as to remind us that even the most basic and common experience of human yearning, the hunger for food, is an indication of our desire for a greater, divine satisfaction. The French Christian mystic, Simone Weil, reckoned along the same lines when she said:

The danger is not lest the soul should doubt whether there is any bread, but lest, by a lie, it should persuade itself that it is not hungry. It can only persuade itself of this by lying, for the reality of hunger is not a belief; it is a certainty.[3]

Likewise, just as hungering after food or sex are certainties, not debatable theories, so the other yearnings for eternity and truth are equally certain. You can only persuade yourself that you don't desire spiritual health by lying to yourself. Lewis goes on:

. . .surely a man's hunger does prove that he comes from a race which repairs its body by eating and inhabits a world where eatable substances exist. In the same way. . . my desire for Paradise. . . is a pretty good indication that such a thing exists. . . A man may love a woman and not win her; but it would be very odd if the phenomenon called 'falling in love' occurred in a sexless world.[4]

Equally, the yearning for God is a pretty good indication he is there. There is a verse in the Psalms that goes like this: 'As the deer pants for streams of water, so my soul pants for you, O God. My soul thirsts for God, the living God.'[5] All hunger has the same root: anchoring our bodies, psyches and spirits to each other. Ecstatic experiences of physical or psychological fulfilment are echoes that there is more and we will never be truly satisfied until we have encountered the More we are seeking. Perhaps the neatest and best known expression of this is found in the famous prayer of St Augustine: 'You made us for yourself and our hearts are restless until they find their rest in you.'[6]

In fact, in his *Confessions*, Augustine expresses this hungering for God with great passion and concludes his verse with a strongly sexual connotation:

Late have I loved you, O Beauty ever ancient, ever new!
Late have I loved you! and behold
You were within, and I without,
  and without I sought You.
And deformed I ran after those forms of beauty
  You have made.
You were with me and I was not with You.
Those things held me back from You,
  things whose only being was to be in You.
You called; You cried;
  and You broke through my deafness.
You flashed; You shone;
  and You chased away my blindness.
You became fragrant;
  and I inhaled and sighed for You.
I tasted,
  and now hunger and thirst for You.

You touched me;
and I burned for Your embrace.[7]

The great Olympic runner and missionary, Eric Liddell, the subject of the film *Chariots of Fire*, used to say that when he ran fast, he felt God's pleasure. For him, physical excellence quite naturally opened doors to spiritual realities.

I don't want to imply that physical exertion necessarily guarantees spiritual renewal. Nor do I want to leave the impression that God can be encountered through the gratifying of physical appetites. This has been the mistake of the pagan religions. But if they are intrinsically related, we cannot seriously examine one without considering the impact on the others. And, as I've already pointed out, an examination of the spiritual aspect of human nature (which includes the sexual) will open doors to the country where God dwells.

So this will be a book about God. And a book about ourselves. A very good combination, I believe.

✠ Human sexuality points us towards God

Let's begin by talking about sex. No, wait a minute. Everyone's talking about sex. Let's talk about sexuality, instead.

Is there a difference, you ask? Well yes, there is, but you wouldn't know it by the way many people, including those in the media, talk. Lots of people use these two terms interchangeably, as if they're the same thing. But they're not the same. And yet they are so completely bound up in each other that you can barely begin to separate them. Everyone's prepared to talk about sex (even when they're calling it sexuality), but no-one, it seems, wants to address the more fundamental questions about human sexuality and gender differences.

Whenever there is a new program on television or the radio that claims it's dealing with 'sexuality', I always tune in. And guess what they're *always* about? Yes, they're dealing with *sex*. They're about 'how to do it', foreplay, safe-sex, penis size, bodies, bodies, bodies. Now, I have no objection to these issues being addressed responsibly in a public forum. What I regret is that they don't do what they claim to do, which is to talk publicly about *sexuality* — about masculinity, about femininity, about relationships, about spirituality. Everyone's talking about sex. Very few people are addressing the more basic issues of sexuality.

We are observing a crisis in our culture that concerns the inadequate formulations we have for understanding our sexuality. Men no longer have clear workable understandings about the way they should relate, as men, to their world. And the same could be said of women. The sexual revolution of the 'sixties and 'seventies was indeed just that — a revolution. It swept away many of our stereotypical and unfair formulations about the roles of men and women and demanded that we look more realistically at our sexuality, as well as our sexual practices. But like most revolutions, it has been followed by a period of chaos and redefinition where the dust is still settling and the more realistic formulations are still bedding down (pardon the pun). We find ourselves in the midst of that chaos.

The difficulty is that during any post-revolutionary chaos, there are always voices calling us back to the old ways, urging us to abandon the advances we have fought for and won. Well, we don't want to go back to the suggestion that men are superior to women, or that they are stronger or more rational or more capable. But by the same token, we're not prepared to swallow a belief that men and women are the *same*. We can see with our own eyes that we're not the same — and I don't just mean physiologically. We are equal, but we're not the same. We respond to certain stimuli in different ways. We see the world differently. We speak in different ways, yearn for different things. The differences may be subtle, but they are unmistakable.

The trick, in order to navigate our way through this chaotic period of redefining our sexual identities, is to work out the ways in which masculinity differs from femininity, without falling into the trap of reproducing equally prescriptive formulae as those we are breaking free of. As theologian Reinhold Niebuhr reminds us: 'Every new freedom represents a new peril as well as a new promise.'

I also believe we need to come clean about the distinctly spiritual nature of human sexuality. Our sexuality is not just about what we do with our bodies. It concerns a very definite religio-spiritual element, tapping into very core human needs and desires and wounds. A healthy and open discussion about human sexuality will inevitably lead us towards the divine, for I strongly believe we are brushed with the 'sexuality' of God.

But we ought not be too optimistic. In lots of ways, our sexual appetite offers an experience of the divine, of transcendence — or alternatively, the very real threat or temptation of the transgressive and the demonic. Human sexuality has been manifest at the root of very great godliness and at the root of very great evil. Such is the nature of spiritual reality. It offers the possibility of both good and ill.

When I use the term 'sexuality' in relation to God, I am using a literary allusion. God is not sexual in the way that we are sexual, male and female. God is neither. And yet he exhibits qualities that are both. Insofar as God's character resembles traits and characteristics that we consider masculine and feminine, we are able to say that, in *certain respects*, God is masculine and feminine. But more on this later.

As long as we remain aware of this paradoxical reality — that an embracing of our sexuality and its relationship to our spirituality can have either divine or demonic repercussions — we should proceed with caution. The church has historically been greatly concerned about the evils of human sexuality and spirituality — and fair enough. My concern is that that has not been a balanced approach. It's time we rediscovered the divine spirituality of human sexuality. It's true that dreadful suffering has occurred to, or at the hands of, those who have expressed their sexual appetites in transgressive ways. But that need not necessarily be the reason for the abandonment of the other side of the coin.

It might help us focus on positive aspects of sexuality by looking at the distinctions between sex and sexuality.

Talking about sex is easy (and now very acceptable), because it's far easier than dealing with the tougher questions regarding human sexuality. How can I define them differently? Well, from the outset I have to be careful. It was Einstein who said we should make everything as simple as possible, but not more so. If I simplify these two concepts too greatly or too tritely, I run the risk of losing the essence of their complexity.

When we talk about sex, we are generally discussing our bodiliness or genitality — the way bodies and genitals fit together. We are dealing with the technique and practicalities of sexual experience and the physiology involved. When we talk about sexuality, we deal with something deeper, something spiritual, something even more integral to humanness.

Watch when you raise a discussion on sex practices and you'll generally observe that most people are articulate and prepared to tackle the questions head on. But ask the same questions about masculinity and femininity and watch people blanch. We all know how penises and vaginas work and how they fit together. But many of us don't have adequate answers for what makes men masculine or women feminine.

We have to awaken to the necessary distinction between sexuality and sex/genitality. Whilst ever we assume that sexuality and genitality are exactly the same, the narrowness of our definition restricts any genuine opportunity for a creative integration of sexuality and spirituality — the road to human wholeness.

By 'sexuality', I mean that essential, all-pervasive complementarity between persons and, in a certain sense, between all living things. Life is attracted to life. Beauty is attracted to both beauty and brokenness — which is a pretty good description of all that lives. This is sexuality. It is our energy for life and communication. Without it, we would settle for a cold, metallic kind of life; we would all be trapped in our own inner world with no need to reach out, no desire to care.

Genitality is a specific expression of our sexual selves. Theologian Emil Brunner says: 'Our sexuality penetrates to the deepest metaphysical ground of our personality. As a result, the physical differences between the man and the woman are a parable of the psychical and spiritual differences of a more ultimate nature.'[8]

I find this a useful way of looking at the relationship between our genitality and our sexuality. The former is a 'parable' of the latter. Our genitality hints at and gives clues to the essence of our sexuality. Our genitality is that strictly biological and anatomical complementarity associated with the sexual organs and with the primary sexual characteristics. It cannot be treated as being the sum of our sexuality, but at the same time will never be understood unless we have first been accepted as and have grown as sexual men and women. Much current discussion completely misses the boat when it cuts to the chase and simply deals with human sexual practice.

To be accepted and grow as sexual beings, we have to recognise that our sexuality includes the entire range of feelings and behaviours which humans have and use as physical and emotional beings. As D.H. Lawrence once said: 'Sex isn't something you've got to play with; sex is you! It's the flow of your life, it's the moving self and you are due to be true to the nature of it. . .'

Our sexuality embodies those feelings and behaviours we have which express relationship with ourselves and others through look, touch and action. And I would include God in the category of 'others'. Our sexuality includes the unique combination of our gender (our identity and role), sex (our anatomy and physiology) and personality (spirituality). So sexuality includes, but is much more than just sex. As Catholic theologian Joan Timmerman says: 'Human sexuality encompasses intention, respect and intimacy that go beyond and sometimes stop short of the act by which the woman's vagina contains the man's penis.'[9]

Clearly, sexuality is a complex reality. It entails the phenomenon of the psyche — emotions, dreams, hopes, expectations, fears, memories, images and self-concept. Many people now agree that this dimension of sexuality is the more important in human beings — even when only satisfying a sex drive is the main concern. Those who are desperately searching for nothing but good sex in a relationship are increasingly being viewed negatively.

But there is even more. The attractions and repulsions experienced in sexuality are indicators of value. They speak of love and hate, of honesty and dishonesty. Essentially, sexuality is concerned with the issues of truth and value. These are spiritual realities. Let's be frank from the outset; sexuality and spirituality are close bedfellows. Says theologian, James Nelson: 'Movement towards a more healed, holistic spirituality and movement towards a more healed, holistic sexuality cannot be separated. It is not that they just ought not be separated;

quite literally they cannot be. One is necessary for the other.'[10]

Spirituality has been described as the conversation — sometimes interrupted, sometimes lively, but always ongoing — with that Unknown with which the known is connected. It's what we reach for when, in music or art or love or sport or work, we aim for *more*. Our spirituality is the response of the whole person — body, mind, feelings, relationships. So conceptualising spirituality in its fullest reality should include sexuality and vice versa. They are both indications of human wholeness.

In the Old Testament, the term for 'spirit' is the Hebrew term *ruah*. It can be quite literally translated as 'wind' or 'breath' or 'breeze', but it implies much more. In effect, it is the wind that activates life, that moves and motivates living things towards vitality. The spirit of God in creation is described as a 'mighty wind' in Genesis 1, verse 2 and includes the giving of the 'breath of life' to humankind. It means more than life. Our bodies will function perfectly well as they were intended, but without the *ruah* they are like a cold, metallic machine, efficient and soulless. God's maintenance of 'spirit' in things or persons is that which sustains their existence as *living* things.

Sex could be a cold, technical, machine-like activity of human bodies without the *ruah*. With it, sex is more than genitality — it is the enriching experience of human sexuality. But before you think anything spiritual should give you a positive, warm inner glow, remember that the 'spirit' of humankind is just as likely to be experienced in negative ways. Because we are spiritual beings, we have tasted bitterness, jealousy, anguish, grief, anxiety and anger. But we are also able to experience trust, truth, honesty, commitment, compassion, excellence, wisdom and faithfulness. Our experience of sex is likely to have drawn to the surface any number of these spiritual realities.

Spiritual teacher, Sam Keen, has put it well when he says:

> No human activity is so surrounded [as sex is] with glory and baseness, so full of divine promise and demonic powers. It may be the ultimate sacrament, the spiritual union of man and woman. . . or it may be the degraded humping of anonymous bodies. It may be praised in gossamer lyrics or reduced to pornographic grunts. It may be a path that leads to beatific union or to pandemonium.[11]

So, like anything which holds so much promise, there are great risks involved. Our sexuality is so powerful and must therefore be handled with great care. Our sexuality can at times be a great blessing and at other times a great source of pain. Because it is such a powerful device for connection with others and an intrinsic part of the spiritual makeup of the human being, whenever it is damaged, abused or misused the repercussions are enormous.

Those who have been sexually abused as youngsters, or whose sexuality has been misused by uncaring lovers, or who have been raped — even those who have themselves misused their own sexuality — will know the unspeakable damage that is done. Whether misused from within or abused from without, sexual damage is deep, very deep. Our sexual woundedness, though, can itself be a pointed and useful (if unwelcome) indicator to even greater realities than those we see around us at first glance.

If our sexuality is really just what we do with our bodies, why does it hurt so damn much when it is betrayed, scorned or violated? The simple answer is because it's not just something we do with our genitals. It's about our very personality — it's about us. When you violate my need for sleep, I will be annoyed, but not wounded. When you violate my sexuality, you damage me. That's because my sexuality is not just a physical craving. It's the echo of an unheard tune. It's part of the journey towards God.

In the Bible, the search for God is said to originate in the spirit of a person — as if, when God breathed the *ruah* into human bodies, he infected those bodies with a hunger to be spiritually satisfied by God. All hunger resembles *ruah* hunger. It is insatiable until it finds its origins in God. Remember, as C.S. Lewis claimed, if we find a desire which no experience in this world can satisfy, the most probable explanation is that we are made for another world.

So, when we try to deal with sexuality responsibly and seriously, we must be drawn to ask questions about gender difference *and* about spirituality, God, the universe and the meaning of life. In fact, developing a healthy awareness of sexuality will draw us closer and closer to the 'other world', to the ultimate realities of existence.

2

MASCULINITY AND FEMININITY

How true love is expressed through gender

The lesson of sex difference research is that men and women are different, but equal. . . With two sexes working together, complementing each other, it can't but be a better, stronger world.

Robert Pool

I know I have the body of a weak and feeble woman, but I have the heart and stomach of a king, and of a king of England, too.

Elizabeth I

AS WE LOOK CAREFULLY AT HUMAN SEXUALITY and the clues it throws up for us in our search for even greater realities, we become inevitably drawn to look at gender differences. If our sexuality is the energy for living, the power of connection, the motivation to communicate as many believe it is, then we need to recognise that it seems to be expressed differently in men and women. So let's examine how that energy called sexuality is expressed through masculinity and femininity.

Whenever you attempt to discuss what makes men

men or women women, you get into trouble. That's because you're forced to make sweeping generalisations that never hold true for every case and always trigger in the people you're talking to exceptions to the rule. Nevertheless, if we're to consider seriously a contemporary approach to understanding our sexuality, we need to at least broach this subject. After all, we are living at a time when the sexes are chiefly differentiated by the view that women should be glamorous and men predatory. Our popular culture, via television, film and music, has not adequately offered us the resources to understand gender differences or our sexuality generally.

✠ Inadequate explanations, past and present, of gender difference

At least we have, in recent times, moved away from the crude and frankly discriminatory generalisations that used to characterise any discussion about gender differences. Even the great thinkers like Philo, Augustine and Thomas Aquinas described femininity as inferior to masculinity. Men were thought of as reasonable and aggressive, while women were seen as emotional and nurturing — characteristics seen as clearly less valuable than masculine traits.

In fact, it was formulated by them that men were associated with *culture* — that is, the area over which humans have control — while women were associated with *nature*, the sphere to which humans were dependent. When a man was deemed to be rational, it naturally followed then that women must be irrational. It has been suggested that from the beginnings of philosophical thought, femaleness was symbolically associated with what Reason left behind.

No-one ever seemed to cotton on to the fact that there were so many notable exceptions to the so-called rule. Rather, these artificial and indefensible distinctions have been embraced and instilled in generation after generation — even to our own generation. This isn't to suggest that there haven't been major and irreversible changes taking place in the latter part of the twentieth century.

Nevertheless, the 'weaker sex' mentality still pervades. We need to be addressing gender relations as a significant sexuality issue. There are too many high school students in this country who know just about everything there is to know about sexual practice, but have no resources for understanding the differences between the masculine psyche and the feminine and how the two interact and affect each other.

Recently, I spoke at a conference for young student leaders from some of the top schools in Sydney. I was retelling the biblical story of the time that Jesus visited the home of two sisters named Mary and Martha. In the story, Mary sits at Jesus' feet as he teaches her while Martha, being the perfect host, dutifully goes off to the kitchen to prepare a meal. In telling the story, I said, 'Now, when Jesus called on the sisters, Martha did what any woman would do when a man came to her home. She proceeded to the. . .'

'Bedroom,' groaned one lusty, male senior, to which every other testosterone-blinded student in the back row growled haughtily. It was a disturbing moment. Some of the young female students in the front rows looked anxious.

I decided to ignore the comment and continued, 'She proceeded to the kitchen.'

'Next best thing,' came the reply. The whole back row of senior boys, aged around sixteen or seventeen, set off a wave of deep gutterel growling. By now I was seeing red. I abandoned what I was planning to say (which had nothing to do with gender issues) and outlined what an affront it was to Jesus to imply he would ever see anyone as being consigned to the bedroom or the kitchen. Warming to my theme, I explained that one of Jesus' greatest points of impact was that he refused to treat anyone — lepers, children, tax-collectors, the poor, the illiterate, the sick — as being of less value than anyone else. He certainly never treated women as second-class citizens. After I'd let them have it, there was an awkward moment of silence before I returned to my prepared presentation.

After the session, and to his credit, the young man from the back row who had made the comments came straight up to me. He apologised for the insensitive remarks and said he was only joking. He didn't mean anything by it. We began to talk about gender issues and gender justice. This young man was seventeen years old. He went to one of the three top boys' schools in the country. As we spoke, he said, 'Listen, I don't know how to treat women as equals. Do you still have to open the car door for them? Is it rude to pay for dinner for them? How does it work nowadays?'

It occurred to me that he wasn't so much a perpetrator of gender injustice, but a victim himself. He quite genuinely had no idea about how men and women should relate in civil social intercourse. I'll bet he knew all about sex. But he knew nothing about masculine and feminine sexuality. At one point, he shook his head incredulously after I described how marriages should work and said with astonishment, 'What you're describing sounds a lot like a partnership!' When the idea of marriage as a partnership is a news flash to a high school boy, we've got problems.

Not that a lot of the current literature is all that helpful in this regard. In a recent book on masculinity, for example, former Green Beret and now Christian minister, Stu Weber, articulates the distinctions between men and women in such a way as to reaffirm the arbitrary and artificial differences mentioned by Augustine or Aquinas:

> Men tend to be tough and strong. Women tend to be tender and gentle.
> A man tends toward logic and linear thinking. A woman tends toward emotional and verbal communication.
> A man tends to be a risk taker, ready to 'go for it'. A woman generally prefers security and order.
> A man tends toward relational insensitivity, a woman toward sensitivity.
> A man looks toward the long haul. A woman is concerned about here and now.
> A man tends to be more sceptical and suspicious (I think it's the protector in him). A woman tends to be more believing and trusting (I think it's the nurturer in her).[1]

When we read these formulations, we have to ask ourselves whether we are considering the basic, core differences between masculinity and femininity or whether we are dealing with culturally prescribed expectations of gender. Is Weber tracking something that clearly offers answers to fundamental questions of sexual identity, or is he selling us a belief that middle America has about the roles of men and women? Surely, some of the arbitrary prescriptions he is offering barely hold water. The suggestion that women aren't up to the long haul is almost too foolish for comment.

Another Christian writer, Gary Smalley, illustrates the differences between men and women with the analogy of the buffalo and the butterfly. For Smalley, men are like the buffalo — tough, lumbering, immovable. They trample flowers and field life under foot as they insensitively amble about in search of food. Women, on the other hand, are like butterflies — flighty, gentle, fragile, fluttering from one flower to the next. The butterfly is sensitive, touching its world ever so daintily. Whereas the butterfly can be blown about hither and yon by every gust of wind, the buffalo is unmoved by even the most ferocious of storms. Tie a pebble to a butterfly and it hits the deck. Attach a pebble to a buffalo and the big, insensitive lug barely notices.[2]

As a man, I am offended by the implications of such a banal illustration (I can't imagine how women must feel about it). It indicates how little many people, including those who dare to write on the subject, know about human sexuality. So Christian writers today, just like those of long ago, can fall into making unhelpful distinctions between masculinity and femininity.

Is it possible, then, to describe adequately the core

differences between men and women? Isn't it entirely inadequate to think that by calling men strong and women gentle, we have tapped the core differences between us? Aren't there enough strong women and gentle men to overturn this childish pronouncement?

So what will do the trick? Since our sexuality, like our spirituality, is about core goals and ultimate meanings, let's begin our search here, by looking at those core goals.

✠ Completeness versus interdependence as core gender differences

According to sociologist, Carol Gilligan, men, when asked to identify their core values and goals and to decide on ultimate meanings, respond by suggesting that they want to develop *completeness*. They say that human maturity means 'feeling strong within yourself', developing confidence, attaining independence. In other words, core masculine goals involve the idea of separation, of mastery and control. For many men, ultimate meanings are based on the individual attaining mastery over his world, becoming the determiner of his own destiny. Those ultimate meanings are expressed powerfully in terms of separation, individualism and achievement.

On the other hand, women, when asked about core values and goals, make reference to developing close relationships, about bonding, about *interdependence*. For women, involvement and attachment are key ideas. Gilligan, in her book, *In A Different Voice*, argues that human beings communicate with others and their environment in very different tongues depending upon their gender. She suggests that while men speak about 'entering their world with impact' or finding 'completeness within oneself', women are far more obviously concerned with attachment to others and enjoying a world of intimate relationships.[3] So our sexuality is about our energy of connection and it is different between men and women.

And Gilligan is not just referring to women who have embraced traditional gender roles, but also to women who have been highly successful in careers outside the home. It seems a successful businessman will define himself in terms of the contracts he has won, the degrees he has earned, the position he has attained. But a similarly successful woman will talk about with whom she has worked, how satisfying the work environment had become, how fulfilling was the interdependence between colleagues.

It's important to note how these differences impact on relationships in Gilligan's research. She found that women see relationships in terms of a web, with family and friends forming a complex set of interconnecting networks. Men view their relationships — particularly with other men — in terms of a hierarchy and always want to know who's on top. Women tend to seek to find common ground, while men prefer to compete with and measure themselves against others.

Gilligan went so far as to claim that in the process of maturation, men and women start at different points and meet somewhere in the middle. Females begin by caring about others, often to the exclusion of themselves, and need to learn to move from an 'others' perspective, back to caring for themselves. Males start off focussed on their own needs and have to learn to think of those around them. We can all think of many friends and acquaintances who haven't moved too far towards the middle.

Gilligan's findings hold true not just in the workplace, but in the home also. A good number of us have grown up with fathers who, whenever we shared our fears, struggles or concerns with them, tried to solve or fix our problem for us. They would ask us how much money we needed or offer to call people to set things straight. They were our aloof, effective Mr-Fix-Its. And there were many times while we were growing up when we needed things being fixed or solved for us.

On the other hand, how did many of our mothers respond when we were in need? Wasn't it altogether differently? Didn't our mothers tolerate not-knowing, not-healing, not-curing? It was our mothers who, instead of giving much advice, solutions or cures, chose to share our powerlessness. Our mothers offered us their support, their loyalty, their presence without feeling they had to fix anything.

I realise I am generalising somewhat, but nevertheless I believe it is a generalisation that the research seems to bear out. The masculine character seems to prefer completeness, solutions, mastery and control. None of these things are necessarily bad in and of themselves. The feminine character offers nurture, presence, attachment, bonding. They speak in different voices.

There has been some considerable research done lately into what's been termed the *Male Answer Syn-*

drome. That is the compulsive male desire to be able to offer an answer or a solution to every question. Haven't you noticed how some guys who've never travelled outside their own country on holidays can tell you all about the Japanese or Korean 'way of thinking'? It seems that there is a chronic fear of appearing ignorant that affects men far more than women. For men, many conversations are not much more than question-and-answer affairs. If your part of the conversation is to provide the answers, you'd jolly well better come up with something. So great is this pressure that for men to admit ignorance can be seen as tantamount to displaying weakness. This could be why men are so afraid to ask directions from strangers, even when hopelessly lost.

Ask any man for his opinion on some geo-political issue of the day, or a technical question on the workings of some device, and he doesn't ask himself whether he knows anything at all about the subject; he simply launches in. Irrespective of his breadth of knowledge (or lack thereof), or of whether or not he has anything interesting to say, a man seems bound to come up with an answer, any answer. The Male Answer Syndrome goes to his greater interest in solutions and control.

In this regard, Caris Davis writes:

If you ask a woman, 'Why do breakfast TV presenters wear those ties?', she will probably shrug helplessly, acknowledging that some things are simply unknowable. A man, on the other hand, will bump those gums: 'They're related to the designer. . . colourblind. . . it's all part of a fascinating strategy of product placement on TV.' Men have the courage and inventiveness to try to explain the inexplicable.[4]

And I think he's right. Rather than perceiving this predeliction for solutions as arrogance or foolishness, let's see it as courageous and inventive.

We have to be careful not to make out that everything feminine is wonderful and everything masculine is not. This is not a fair distinction to draw. But it is reasonable to admit they're different.

Consider the different ways men and women hold their babies. Women hold their babies close; they roll them in on their breast and offer them comfort and security. But have you ever noticed how men hold their babies? They hold them away from their bodies on an extended arm.

We could be forgiven for thinking this is cold and uncaring or unnurturing. But think of it this way; think of it as a father saying to his child, 'Here we are! Here's our world! Stick with me and it's a safe and exciting place.' There's a daring, a boldness associated with this action that's perfectly healthy for a tiny infant to discover. In fact, I think it's every bit as healthy as the experience of a close cuddle.

✠ Louis Nowra's four key aspects of masculinity

In an article, *What Maketh The Man?*, Australian playwright, Louis Nowra, identifies four key aspects to masculinity.

Nowra's first key aspect of masculinity is genitalia. He says you cannot discount its importance in determining what makes a man. It might seem like stating the obvious, but Nowra makes some interesting observations about the effect of male genitalia on the way men relate to their worlds. Sure, it seems so obvious that being born with a penis is what makes you male, but the degree to which that appendage affects your self-image, your encounters with the world, your relationships should not be underestimated.

Larry Crabb, a Christian counsellor, in his book *Men and Women: Enjoying the Difference*, makes something of the 'movements' associated with the ways the masculine and feminine respond to their worlds. While men are concerned with 'entering' their world, 'moving towards' others, 'penetrating' their environments through action and objects, women seem far more interested in 'inviting' others into their world, 'bonding', 'enfolding', 'attaching'. These very subtle distinctions really do belie very interesting differences between men and women.

It was Emil Brunner, we noted earlier, who mentioned that the physical differences between men and women are a parable of the psychological and spiritual differences. In this regard, the act of sexual intercourse involving the man penetrating and entering his partner, and the woman inviting and enfolding hers, is entirely parabolic of far deeper identity roles.

Nowra's second key aspect of masculinity is action. This is, in some ways, related to his first point — men learn to be men by conquering their worlds with their bodies. Says Nowra:

You quickly learn the pleasures of the active body as a way to freedom and how to use your body as a weapon. Running, jumping, throwing, hitting; ---- they all give an exhilarating sense of escaping the world of speech and emotion, into a world where to command your body and make it do what you want it to do is one of your great achievements. There is an exquisite, almost spiritual pleasure in hitting a ball exactly where you want it to go, or running with other boys, straining to beat them, hearing their heavy footsteps, their gasping for breath and knowing their desire to win is as strong as yours.[5]

Even as early as the playground, young boys learn that mastering their small world is the way to wholeness, feeling good and feeling safe. Winning, competing, controlling — these facets to life are intrinsically masculine. Nowra continues:

[There is] a sense of competition and of an aggressive will to dominate, to scare your opponent, to intimidate him. The curious thing was we (the competitors) were still the best of friends afterwards, as if we had instinctively understood that this aggression wasn't personal, but an intrinsic and unavoidable part of ourselves (as male).[6]

In fact, this is a view held by another Australian writer, Tim Winton. While Nowra sees a basic core male desire for action as positive, Winton offers a healthy corrective against imbalance in this regard:

Men have an overwhelming propensity to act. From the cradle, this is what they are taught to do. A boy does not feel, he acts. Three decades of feminism have made almost no impact on such training, and yet it distorts men's lives, deprives them of so much and affects the balance of all

society very much for the worse. Men will allow themselves
to feel only so far.[7]

I believe Winton is correct when he says that the
emphasis on action over and against feeling has historically been a flaw in masculinity. But it's not enough for
us to call men to 'feel' more as if this is something we
should muster up from within ourselves. Masculinity
seems to have a propensity to act. But that's not to say
that we are not able to tease out from within men skills
and interests in pursuing affection. As we'll see later,
the way to human wholeness is for men and women to
discover the qualities they can share in common. In fact,
as we'll see, God shares both 'sets' of characteristics with
us and the key to wholeness is to be more like God.

*Nowra's third key aspect of masculinity is the impor-
tance of objects.* He believes that as boys grow to
manhood, they begin to relate to the world through
objects. For many young boys, these objects are round
— cricket balls, soccer balls, basketballs. But the car
freak, the computer whiz and the chess enthusiast is the
same. Whether it's cameras, guns, war machines or any
type of machinery, these devices are objects a man can
know, manipulate and control.

Ever been around your father or your boss or your
favourite uncle and expressed frustration that a particular
piece of kitchen gadgetry, a computer program or something in your car doesn't work properly? Doesn't he
almost knock you aside to get to the offending piece of
equipment in order to. . . fix it! Those old enough will

remember James Taylor's old masculine anthem: 'I fix broken hearts, baby. I'm your handyman.'

This adoration of objects results in or finds its source in a mode of thinking that's pretty straightforward: a problem is to be solved. Machines or devices can be mended when they don't perform according to expectation or specification. People can't. Here is another strength of being male that can easily become a weakness. People are not objects. A woman is prepared to work through a problem with someone in order to solve it. A man wants to jump immediately to the solution. But life isn't always like that.

It's worth remembering the difference between healing and fixing. To heal is to engage with the client/patient/friend in such a way as to promote health, to overcome obstacles to growth and to tease out the capabilities of the unhealthy to become whole. Healing, whether physical or emotional, involves time, pain, struggle, commitment and, above all, relationship. To fix, on the other hand, is to repair something that no longer functions as intended. It may take time and commitment, but it differs from healing insofar as it doesn't require any engagement between the fixer and the broken. Interestingly, men seem good at fixing *things*, while women respond to healing *others*. This leads us on to Nowra's final point.

Nowra's fourth aspect of masculinity is the distinctive nature of masculine relationships. He suggests that all this 'feeling' stuff currently being foisted onto men is not all that natural. He says: 'There is a tendency now to want men to "express their feelings", yet it is in this very inarticulateness that men sometimes express their deepest emotions.'[8] In fact, he goes so far as to say that the deepest connections men make don't require words. I hope he's not copping out, though I appreciate his corrective.

Maybe some relationships don't need lots of words, lots of analysis. Maybe we need to learn from masculinity in this regard. Some women have learned to control their worlds and those around them with lots of words. Perhaps they need to learn from men to contain their feelings at times, be more silent and let people 'be' a little.

Now, let's be clear from this point that it's notoriously difficult to make clear pronouncements about the nature of femininity and the nature of masculinity. That's why so few people dare to, and those who do often make inadequate pronouncements. The distinction that writers like Larry Crabb, Carol Gilligan and Emil Brunner draw between separateness and togetherness, or entering and inviting, doesn't hold true like some unbreakable cosmic law.

I'm not suggesting for a minute that women are not capable, or even naturally disposed towards, being concerned with separation, with completeness or independence. In fact, as we will see later, the way to human wholeness is by an integration of the masculine and feminine in us all.

Nevertheless, if we can be permitted to speak in generalisations for the time being, I think Gilligan's and

Crabb's findings hold true. As social commentator, Irma Kurtz, writes: 'Men's great fear, I'm sure, is fear of failure. The woman's fear is fear of not being loved.'

✠ Some currently observed gender differences in behaviour and attitude

I want to offer three examples of these differences. The first two examples are from others; the third from my own experience.

In the first two examples, one concerns men performing roles traditionally assigned to women and the other concerns women performing roles traditionally assigned to men.

In a recent survey of the nursing profession, it was revealed that male nurses conducted themselves and performed their duties in different ways to female nurses. It was also revealed that male and female nurses had differing views on the way each fulfilled their role. Remember that this has been a profession traditionally dominated by women. Today, only ten per cent of nursing staff are men. According to the study, presented to the International Nursing Research Congress held in Sydney in 1994, while men and women nurses credited one another with high levels of education and competence, women gave less praise to the caring and nurturing qualities of their male colleagues.

Interestingly, male nurses, when asked about the nature of the caring profession, interpreted caring in an objective, detached and pragmatic sort of way — meeting patients' needs. Female nurses also felt committed to meeting patients' needs, but were equally committed to being more intuitive, emotional and nurturing about it. According to the study, ambition, confidence, assertiveness and technical ability were at the top of the list of attributes considered highly desirable by male nurses. They identified themselves as particularly technical, professional, logical, assertive and decisive. But neither male nor female nurses listed these qualities in their women peers.

So even when engaging in what has been traditionally (if unfairly) seen as a female career, men exhibit very distinct characteristics in fulfilling such a role. In fact, the average male nurse speaks in a 'different voice' and has a different energy of life and communication and connection to the average female nurse. Once again, Gilligan's suggestions regarding core values seem to hold true. The 'movements' of the male nurse seem to be different from the female nurse. The men appear to be concerned with achievement and mastery over their world. The women are interested in bonding and developing an attachment to their patients. The study clearly stated that this in no way indicated that the quality of care offered to patients by male nurses was inferior to that offered by female nurses. It was just different.

The second example concerns the relatively new innovation of having women journalists acting as war correspondents. Historically, there has been a greater acceptance of female writers reporting from the front of a major battle than there has been of male nurses. But there is now no longer any stigma attached to this being a male vocation. Anne Deveson, a feminist social commentator, has highlighted the differing ways in which men and women report on war.

Deveson suggests that the increasingly disturbing and graphic way that war is presented in the media has to do with the greater number of women journalists, camera operators and photographers reporting from the front. She believes that when war was chiefly presented by male journalists, there was a greater concern for reporting on the 'big picture'. Male writers were interested in detailing strategy, the state of play, who's winning and who's losing. The electronic media was quick to present images of guns and tanks and planes, and pictures of generals planning in the war room.

However, with an increasing number of women reporting from the front has come a greater concern for detailing the human face of conflict. Female journalists and photographers have been committed to exposing the carnage of war. Female reporters have exposed the devastating effects of war, such as starvation and homelessness. Women at the front have forced us to look at images of orphanages, crowded to overflowing without enough food or bed clothes. And they have brought to international attention the unspeakable crime of war rape. So together, male and female reporters will tell the whole truth, offering both sides of the sorry story.

Deveson's view is that while men are interested in what a war is achieving, women are wanting to champion those victims to whom they have become attached. Nowhere has this been more apparent than in the civil war in what was once Yugoslavia. The Serbian-Bosnian conflict was reported with a more human face than just about any war in recent history. While many members of the public complained that war correspondence in the electronic media was becoming too explicit, too heart-rending, Deveson claims this indicates the difference between men and women as journalists. Men are concerned with separation, women with attachment.

This highlights what we have already noted about gender differences. (In fact, when discussing this recently with a colleague, he ventured that this might explain why women go to public toilets in groups, while men go individually, even though the urinal is a perfect opportunity for male bonding.)

Robert Pool, in his book *The New Sexual Revolution*, outlines how he was visiting the psychology department of a major American university and noticed that the majority of its faculty were men. Knowing that about sixty per cent of people earning PhDs today are women, he wondered what explained this anomaly. One of the few female psychologists on the faculty answered him. Among PhD psychologists, she explained, women are more likely to go into clinical psychology where they can help people, while more men choose to go into psychological research. He quotes her: 'Women are making very different choices than men and it relates to differences in preferences and values,' she said. 'Women are drawn to people-oriented fields, men towards objects.'[9] Note his use of the term 'preferences'. Men and women have different preferences and this need not have any qualitative value attributed to it. Neither one is better or worse, right or wrong. Just plain different!

And, of course, at a much gentler, smaller level, we

observe this difference around us every day. Recently, the school that my daughters attend held a dance. My children are only very young, so I took them — and found it very exciting to attend my girls' first disco.

When we arrived, my daughters were swamped by their friends. A small crowd of girls moved around the room like an amoeba swallowing up any lone girls. It literally enveloped my daughters and they all excitedly compared what each of them was wearing and spoke of how wonderful the whole night was going to be.

One of my good friends arrived shortly after us. He has sons only. When he walked in the door of the school auditorium, I noticed an intriguing thing. As his sons entered the room, they were greeted by their friends. A small crowd of boys moved towards them and began to wrestle them to the ground. There was a gentle skuffle on the floor as several boys held my friend's sons in headlocks and others kneed them in the back. This strange greeting seemed to be conducted without malice. It was their masculine way of connecting. When it was over, they proceeded to greet the next boy to arrive in a similar fashion.

As my daughters moved around the room in a pack, incorporating new arrivees with squeals of delight, the boys continued the biffo on the floor. In fact, several of these wrestling-style greetings had to be broken up when they got out of hand.

I have a friend who reckons that boys come out of primary school having learnt how to kick a ball and each other and girls come out socialised to take on the world. But is this a comment on the school system or a reflection on the basic differences between males and females? I grant you that our school system may need some work, but perhaps this lies in determining ways that we can teach boys to express masculine traits in a more positive fashion.

The implications of this kind of learning process on the extraordinarily high levels of domestic violence is notoriously difficult to track. Boys might come out of school having learnt how to kick balls and other boys, but have they also learnt that it's acceptable to display connection through violence, even violence they may see as playful? And while girls might look socialised to take on the world, why have so many women had such difficulty dealing with violent men?

In this ever so small way, I observed these two profound and basic human movements. The feminine seems to invite, draw in, envelope. The masculine competes, achieves, extends himself, penetrates. How intriguing that this manifests itself so early in our lives.

Again, I want to sound a cautionary note. I am not wanting to develop more of the inadequate formulations that have dogged male-female relations for millenia. I don't wish to reinforce the old furphy that girls are more 'social' than boys.

It's clear that males and females are equally interested in being around other people and that in childhood girls do not spend more time with playmates than boys do. It's the *way* that boys and girls interact with each other that seems to be directed by the sexual 'movements' of which Larry Crabb speaks.

✠ Robert Pool and differences in the way males and females think

Much study has gone into attempting to show that men and women literally don't think alike. Recent studies of human brain function have suggested there is a difference in the way men and women process information. Much was made of this in the stimulating and controversial book, *BrainSex*, by Anne Moir and David Jessel, and the more recent *The New Sexual Revolution* by Robert Pool.

Pool suggests that the differences are marked out hormonally within the womb and that these hormonal differences are as clear as the physiological differences between male and female bodies. In fact, he believes that the combination of hormones and different brain function sets in train features relating to our worlds that are distinctly male or female.

In the first decade of life, he believes, girls are more interested in people, boys in things; girls mature faster, boys engage in more rough and tumble play; and the sexes choose different types of toys to play with. At play, young girls are more focussed on what they're doing, spending more time at an activity and being more likely to finish, while boys are more easily distracted, get bored with an activity more quickly and often drop what they're doing before they complete it.

Later in childhood, boys prefer more complex, structured games, particularly those with clear winners and losers, while girls choose less complex, more cooperative and less competitive activities. In adulthood, men are more aggressive, women more nurturing, women more interested in how well they do a job and men more concerned with their performance relative to others.

Even at a moral-ethical level males, according to Pool, are more likely to base decisions on a set of rules for determining right and wrong, while females tend to consider the personal consequences for the people involved. In conversation, women seek to make connections, while men exchange information and establish their positions relative to others.

Recently, I heard of an experimental role play conducted by therapists who invited couples to pretend they were having the following conversation. The woman was to tell her partner that her mother was coming to stay for a week and that she was taking time off work to be with her. She was to ask her partner if he minded his mother-in-law coming to stay and whether he would be a little more available during the week to spend time with them. The man was not allowed to respond with anything other than nods or noises of affirmation, indicating that he understood what she was saying.

Then the roles were reversed and the man was to relay the same information to his partner, explaining that his mother was coming and asking his wife whether she could be more available to help out with the arrangement. Again, the woman could only affirm that she understood what her partner had said. She could respond in no other way. After each partner had completed the exercise, they were asked how they felt about the exchange. Without fail, all the men were perfectly happy. They had relayed the necessary information and, since their partners hadn't baulked at the idea, they assumed everything should proceed as discussed.

But the women were decidedly unhappy. They found the conversation entirely unsatisfactory. They expressed their need for feedback. They needed to know how their partners *felt* about the suggestion and whether they were supportive of the idea. Nods and grunts were not enough. And this illustrates the point; men are satisfied to fire off the information and imagine that the deed had been done. Women are more likely to be interested in the connections or disconnections that communication causes. It has been summarised by one psychologist in this way: men are happy to *report*, while women desire *rapport!* Columnist Caris Davis reckons that women talk to cement relationships, while men perceive talk to be a form of display. For women, communication is a two-way process coupled with listening. But for men, the opposite of talking isn't listening; it's waiting.

Pool is not suggesting that these sex differences are completely fixed in biology. The most that our biology can do is establish predispositions which interact with the environment to create a person. Nevertheless, he makes a strong case for the impact of hormones in determining those predispositions.

I think it would have to be said that, in spite of the enormous amount of material he canvasses in his book, Pool is still on thin ice to claim too strong a case in this regard. There is an enormous overlap in tests of mental capacities in men and women. So, while there might be some basis for suggesting that brain function is different between the sexes due to genetic differences, there's nothing to indicate that there are characteristics inherent to male or female brains that limit intellectual achievement. At the very best, we may say that male brain function *could* be different from female brain function, but the jury is definitely still out on this one.

✠ Thomas Bever and gender differences in spatial awareness

A recent *Time* magazine article cast some light on the most intriguing of differences in male/female brain function. It claimed, based on the work of psychologist Thomas Bever at the University of Rochester, that men and women have very different degrees of spatial awareness.

His findings will confirm all the frustrations men and women have felt with members of the opposite sex when driving in a new part of town with the help of a street directory. Men and women find their ways around unknown areas very differently. Women tend to rely on landmarks to locate themselves in a new place, while men construct a mental picture or 'map' made up of 'vectors', indicating distance and direction from one point to another.

Using computer maps in his research, women got hopelessly lost when familiar landmarks were removed. Taking away the sun and moon bothered the women also, though it hardly affected the men. But when Bever changed the dimensions of the map by lengthening or shortening various 'corridors', the men got lost, while the women were unaffected.

In another related experiment, Bever had men and women walk around a physical maze several times until they were certain they were thoroughly familiar with its dimensions and shape. He then showed the candidates eight maps of mazes, some of which looked nothing at all like the maze they had just negotiated. It was their task to choose the map that corresponded with the maze through which they had just walked several times.

Eighty-seven per cent of the males got it right, but only twenty-five per cent of the females did. Bever concluded that maps are really a 'male thing'.

So next time you're lost in the car with your spouse somewhere, hand the street directory to *him!* But it also adds weight to those who claim the differences between men and women are basically genetic or physical differences in brain function.

When looking at views like Pool's, it is worth bearing in mind that many would disagree with his (and others') view that men and women are born with such differences. Many believe that people *develop* them as a matter of course through social conditioning. Hormones may push males or females in different directions, but society can either exaggerate or dampen these differences, depending on how we teach our children and what we expect of ourselves. In other words, little boys are given guns, cars and Power Rangers and little girls are offered dolls and tea sets. Men take their sons to the footy and their daughters to ballet classes. Children's books and television programs depict girls playing 'house' and boys wreaking havoc. And all this is true.

Listen to the rhymes children sing in school playgrounds. When I was a child, we used to get the line that little girls were made of 'sugar and spice and all things nice', while boys were just a bundle of 'frogs and snails and puppy dogs' tails'. It seemed cute at the time. Today, you'll hear little girls singing:

> *Girls are handy, made outta candy.*
> *Boys are spastic, made outta plastic.*
> *Girls come from Mars, because they're stars.*
> *Boys come from Jupiter, because they're stupider.*

While much gender difference is socially reinforced in this way, it is also true that many politically correct parents who have worked stringently against promoting any gender bias in their children find themselves amazed at how naturally they adopt the 'movements' we have outlined as soon as they hit school (or even earlier).

✠ Carl Jung and the realisation of our gender potential

It was psychologist, Carl Jung, who proposed a psychological answer that seemed to cover the bases more successfully than either the physiological or sociological answers outlined above. He described the human psyche as being made up of the conscious and the unconscious, with consciousness being the smaller part. He then identified two layers of the unconscious. In the layer closer to the conscious, the *personal* unconscious, are stored the thoughts, memories, impressions, feelings of which we are consciously aware.

The deeper layer, which Jung called the *collective*

unconscious, is formed by heredity and history. Our inherited psychic material exists in the collective unconscious as patterns which Jung called 'archetypes'. We are particularly interested in two of the archetypes Jung identified with the masculine and feminine forms of the Latin word for 'spirit': the *animus* and the *anima*.

Now, Jung was a little cagey about defining these archetypes, but he was prepared to discuss how they manifest themselves in human beings. He believed that every human had, within his or her collective unconscious, *both* these archetypes, but that, depending on your gender, the one or the other would be dominant. In other words, one would be closer to the consciousness of an individual and the other would be deeper within the unconscious.

He suggested that the *anima* tends to be relational, to be inviting of others, to move towards wholeness and appreciate values. It is intuitive, compassionate and emotional. The *animus*, on the other hand, functions logically, appreciates objective facts and recognises interconnections between them; it analyses and discriminates. It sometimes appears competitive, aggressive and unemotional. In other words, boiling it all down, the characteristics we identify as either masculine or feminine appear to come from the level of the unconscious where the *anima* and *animus* reside.

Now remember that Jung suggests we *all* have *both* the *anima* and *animus*. We all have both archetypes built into our psyches. But we manage to contain one and unleash the other, depending on our gender. Therefore, as a man I am more consciously aware of my *animus*, my so-called masculine traits, but I also have the potential to unleash my *anima*, those traits usually considered feminine which dwell deeper below the surface.

And I think this is borne out in my life. While I exhibit many of the functions of the *animus*, I have the capacity to be nurturing or to be intuitive. Those characteristics do lie *deeper* within me, but they are there. I have observed them in my life.

When our first child was born while I was doing undergraduate studies in theology and Carolyn was still working to support us, I noticed very strong nurturing, relational, emotional characteristics coming to the fore in my care for our young baby. I amazed myself at how happily I was able to adopt childcare as a major part of my responsibility — changing nappies, watching Sesame Street, feed times, sleep times. When I recall those days, I often have to ask myself where those nurturing characteristics have gone today.

Jung, and now other psychologists, tell us that the way to wholeness — to a balanced, healthy personality — lies in recognising and allowing all positive qualities to emerge from the unconscious. True psychological health is indicated (at least, in part) by the preparedness of an individual to express his or her dominant archetype in appropriate and creative ways, as well as to foster and tease out the less dominant archetype closer and closer to the surface. The integration of positive feminine and masculine qualities, whether from the conscious or the unconscious, is one of the keys to human wholeness. Being able to connect with others in both ways is holistic sexuality.

Of course, many people are afraid to even admit, let

alone express, opposite-sex personality traits. They do everything in their power to suppress them when they appear from the unconscious. In a recent, very telling ABC documentary on masculine sexuality, *Sex, Guys and Videotape*, it was revealed that many Australian men had absolutely no mechanisms for coping in difficult circumstances. When asked to whom did they turn in times of crisis, most of the prominent personalities interviewed indicated that they had no-one to reach out to.

They even went so far as to say that it was not very masculine to share deeply about personal issues. Several men said they couldn't even tell their wives or girlfriends if they were struggling emotionally. It was considered 'un-masculine' to develop connections and networks of interdependence.

When the members of the gold medal-winning Oarsome Foursome rowing team were asked how they would respond if one of their mates tried to tell them about a deep personal problem, they responded blankly with, 'I guess we'd have to listen to him.' So rare is it for men to attach themselves to others that they have no idea of how to respond when someone attempts to connect with them. If it's considered 'sissy' or 'girlie' to connect emotionally, we have greater cause for concern than you might think.

Young men need to recognise that while competing, achieving, winning, completing might be natural things for them to strive for, it is entirely healthy for them to tease out aspects like bonding and nurturing that might not normally come naturally. It's not enough to just know about sexual technique, about stimulating genitals, about male and female orgasm. And young women need to recognise that while bonding, connecting and nurturing come quite naturally, they can work at learning containment, producing, completing. We need some paradigms for understanding human sexuality, something sadly lacking in our culture today.

What might that paradigm look like? Well, if we are to agree with Carl Jung that the way to human wholeness is by an integration of both masculine and feminine archetypes within each individual, then we need to see what such an integrated being might look like. We need a template or a model. The 'sensitive new age guy' has become a bit of a joke lately. SNAGS are men who can cook pasta, wear pastels and florals, respect a woman's freedom, take No for an answer and cry in sad movies.

Isn't there more to human integration than the adoption of some socially acceptable external practices? Isn't our sexuality about more than things we *do*? Isn't it about *who* we are? Well, who are we to be? What might a healthy integrated sexuality, whether masculine or feminine, look like? Christians for centuries have claimed that the goal of human existence is to imitate God, to become more like him. It's my view also that the Christian idea of God, in fact, provides us with the template we require in the work of being healthy sexual beings.

It's a fundamental Christian belief that humankind was created by God in his image. In other words, we are meant to reflect God's nature. We have fallen dreadfully short of this mark throughout human history, but one of the most persistent beliefs in the Judeo-Christian world view is that we, to quote Joni Mitchell, 'have got to get back to the garden'. We have to return to our roots, if you will. Humankind can only find fulfilment to the degree that they reflect the nature of the one from whom they came. We can see this in various ways. Our desires for justice, mercy, peace, faith and love are all desires to reflect God's nature. But my point is that we mustn't leave our sexuality behind in this regard.

God, as we will see, reflects the sexual 'movements' of humankind. It's perfectly legitimate to see that he exhibits both masculine and feminine traits, and that he is the model of the most exquisitely integrated being. He is both *anima* and *animus*. He is a complete and perfect image of what we yearn for so desperately. God and his human reflection, Jesus, form the paradigm we need for a healthy sexuality. We need to get back to the garden and rediscover the degree to which the divine offers us the resources for integration and wholeness.

3

SEXUALITY AND SPIRITUALITY
How true human and divine love are linked

*A renewed, creative and fully personal fulfilment of
sexuality will only come from people who are aware of
the pressure of a debilitated civilisation and, without con-
tracting out of it, can put down roots in an alternative
culture. Christianity is such a culture.*

V.A. Demant

*Sexuality and spirituality are not, of course, exactly the
same thing. They are not identical twins, but they are
kissing cousins. . .*

M. Scott Peck

SEXUALITY IS ABOUT BASIC HUMAN 'MOVEMENTS' like
penetration and invitation, like separateness and togetherness, like entering and enfolding. These reflect the
physical movements involved in sexual behaviour. But
there's more. The link between our sexuality and our
spirituality is an area of human life that is even more
rarely explored than gender differences.

If we can say that the fundamental differences between masculinity and femininity are reflective of sexual

practice, what underlies this at an even deeper, more spiritual level? Prepare yourself, for when we explore the link between sexuality and spirituality, we are on a journey towards God.

In Western civilisation, sexuality and spirituality have commonly been thought to be antagonistic. In fact, this has been a view generally bouyed up and supported by the church. But the times they are a'changin'. A lot of recent writing and theological and biblical scholarship has raised the possibility of acknowledging a reconciliation of the two, thereby opening the way for a more realistic discussion of healthy attitudes towards sex. More and more ministers are beginning to realise that God created sex and didn't say, 'Oops!', but pronounced sex and the rest of created order as good.

✠ The Bible and sexuality

There's no doubt from the creation story in the Book of Genesis that the recurring motif is 'And God saw that it was good. . .' From the first chapter of the Old Testament, there is no ambivalence about sex. The sexual potency of all earth's creatures is in continuity with the creativity of God. And there is no doubt or ambivalence towards sexuality. God created humans, both male and female.

The creation of humankind as male and female did not entail any hierarchy of genders. On the contrary, male and female were created mutually and equally as the image-bearers of God, responsible to God for the well-being of the creation, each as a biological and social complement of the other. When John Milton, in *Para-*

dise Lost, has Adam ask God to make him a companion, he explicitly insists on an equal, for only an equal can be a true friend. She must also be different, because love cannot be mere self-reflection. Genesis 2 reinforces this point when it says, 'It is not good that the man should be alone' (verse 18). In fact, this verse says that woman was created to be a 'helper fit for' the man.

A much misquoted phrase, this has a very different connotation to our use of the word 'helper'. We would consider a helper to be an assistant to the worker, but the Bible actually ascribes this term to God himself. In such passages as Deuteronomy 33, verse 7 and Psalm 33, verse 20, God is called our 'helper', so it couldn't designate inferiority at all. Nor does it refer to subordination. In the original Hebrew, the phrase 'a helper fit for' suggests an equal and well-matched counterpart rather than a subordinate one.

I'll go so far as to say that these opening words of the Old Testament set in train an approach to sex and sexuality in the Bible that is very positive and conducive to healthy spirituality. Actually, it's considered part of the brokenness of humanity that, after the fall of Adam and Eve, God cursed them in Genesis 3, verse 16 with the pathetic ramifications of their choice: 'Your desire shall be for your husband and he shall rule over you.'

Remember that this is a curse. God has condemned human unfaithfulness by cursing them with such an unequal relationship. Here we see, expressed by the sages of Israel millennia ago, the very gender difference theory we have just been discussing. Women desire connection ('your desire shall be for your husband') and men are into rule and control ('and he shall rule over you'). For my money, this sums up women's pain so thoroughly. It indicates the root of the struggle women have had with codependency, emotional addictions and their preparedness to stay in abusive relationships. It also points out the root of men's anguish over their need for power and control. What is that root? The Judeo-Christian thinkers called it 'sin'.

According to the old creation storytellers, it was never God's original intention for women to desire connectedness so much that they would sacrifice personal autonomy or dignity to get it. It was never God's intention that men would behave abusively or violently to maintain control of his world. This unequal relationship was the result of human sin. It is the result of a broken world and something to be worked against.

Those who claim they are working to 'get the world back to the way God intended it to be' need to recognise that gender equality has to be part of that agenda. A positive, healthy approach to sexuality was an integral feature of the Hebrew creation stories. In fact, it wasn't until after the Christian church had emerged and become the state-endorsed religion in the fourth century that strongly negative attitudes towards sexual expression began to develop. The origins of these attitudes can be tracked back to the dynamic interaction of the Jewish, Greek and Christian traditions which formed our culture. So let's embark on a little potted history.

As we just noted, in the Jewish biblical tradition, sex and human sexuality is the creation of God and it is good. One of its prime functions is to continue the family lineage and so to propagate Israel. This initial Judaistic attitude was welcoming and affirming. However, negative restrictions arose when Israel encountered the orgiastic religious practices among the Canaanites and others in the Promised Land of Palestine. To keep Israel's religion (and blood line) pure, the 'holiness code' of Leviticus — especially the eighteenth chapter, for example — forbade sexual practices associated with pagan rites.

Remember that religious and geneological concerns, not sexual-ethical ones, were at stake. The Christian church, when it finally emerged after Christ, was to inherit this basically positive attitude towards sexuality from Judaism with some fairly decisive qualifications. But this was nothing compared with the profound impact that Hellenisation was to have.

When Greek culture dominated the ancient world, it left its mark on every culture it conquered, Jewish included. The earliest Greeks held that sexual abstinence is a prerequisite for sublime purity. This view influenced Greek philosophers like Plato and Aristotle, who in turn had a great influence on subsequent sexual attitudes. Later, Stoic philosophy prized the soul rather than the body and sex was tolerated for procreation only. Asceticism and self-denial were thought to be the only way to true perfection. This is called dualistic thinking — where the spirit is viewed as basically good and the body as evil. It was believed that the body must be beaten and denied in order to free the purity of the spirit. This was not a Jewish way of thinking at all. And, as we've noted, it's not a healthy way to understand human nature.

Jesus arrived on the scene when Palestine was caught with an uncomfortable coalition of both Jewish and Greek attitudes towards sexuality. He shattered many of the excesses of Hellenisation and reaffirmed a basically Judaistic approach to sexuality, esteeming gender differences in the most positive fashion and promoting freedom and responsibility. He reminded us of the interrelationship between body, soul and spirit. He embraced a healthy and liberated physical lifestyle as well as being intensely religious, a trick not often emulated these days.

Jesus came announcing the sovereignty of God and calling people back to the agenda with which God began. He actualised this in his unconventional and very anti-patriarchal treatment of women. He rejected the reduction of women to their reproductive roles and included them in the circle of those he taught and healed. We will explore Jesus' uncommon approach in a later chapter.

✠ The Christian church down the ages and sexuality

The very early days of the Christian church saw the concerns of Jesus carried on. It adopted a baptismal tradition that initiated both men and women in the faith community (unheard of in those days) and radically ignored gender distinctions, preferring the equality of those 'in Christ'.

Nevertheless, in the following years of Christianity, more and more Christians mistakenly followed the Stoics and began to insist that sexuality conform to the laws of nature which, understood in the narrowest sense, would limit sexual activity to situations in which procreation was intended. Like the Stoics, they felt drawn to resolve how one could be spiritually perfect in the light of an inescapable dependence on food and sexual expression. Not that we die without sex as we do without food, but the need for sexual expression, both bodily (whether by intercourse or masturbation) and psycho-spiritually (the need to connect, communicate, interact), is so clearly overpowering that they believed it to be a matter of dependence.

Was such a dependence not hampering in the quest for purity? To be freed of need and desire was the human ideal articulated by a Jewish sect called the Essenes as well as the Stoics. Since appetite grows even as it is fed, sex and food stood as symbols of humiliation to those who defined being human as being beyond physical desire.

And so extreme ascetic practices, in no way taught by Jesus, continued to abound in Christianity. The Christian leader, Augustine, was foremost in this stream of thinking. Before he converted to Christianity, he was a devotee of Manicheism, an explicit dualistic sect which stressed the essential evil of anything physical, especially sex, something that caused the robust Augustine considerable anguish and guilt. Far from abandoning this philosophy when becoming a Christian, he brought over with him the worst aspects of dualism.

Nevertheless, Augustine himself clearly enjoyed sleeping with a woman. In fact, he opted for the next best thing to marriage — a strictly monogomous relationship with a concubine. This kind of relationship was quite common in intellectual circles. It was seen as an acceptable and often openly acknowledged sexual relationship, not covered by the law, but with a few rules of its own. The chief feature it lacked, considered essential in legal marriage, was the expressed intention to produce legitimate offspring — and Augustine is credited with articulating the belief that sexual relations were best seen as being for the purpose of procreation!

Now Augustine might have chosen his partner because he loved her, but he slept with her because he loved to do so, not to produce children. Since they had only one child in thirteen years, it seems likely Augustine and his concubine practised some kind of birth control.

The pervasive influence of his dualism is evident in Augustine's writings and his personal impact on Christianity to this day is beyond measure. It appears in Medieval Christianity's belief that sexual abstinence is spiritually superior to marriage. Even as late as the Victorian era, this dualism is evident in the general notion that sexual activity and even sexual impulses were a moral threat to be held in suspicion. People thought it 'Christian' to suppress sexual feelings and information about sex.

The dramatic increase in research on sexuality in the first half of this century greatly influenced individual thinking and attitudes and helped ease personal restrictions. Catalysed by the experiences of the 'sixties, a time known as the 'sexual revolution', some religious bodies re-examined their positions on sexual ethics and their approaches to sexuality as a whole. For example, in 1965 at the Second Vatican Council, the Roman Catholic church officially sanctioned a more affirming approach to sexuality. Whereas formerly procreation was considered the primary purpose of sex within a marriage, now a more re-creative aspect was adopted. Sex within marriage was seen as promoting intimacy, pleasure and enjoyment of another and stood as an essential expression of maleness or femaleness.

Further, humanist psychology and the holistic health movement have influenced the contemporary view so that sexuality and spirituality can now be seen not as polarities, but rather as two sides of the one coin. This lands us right in the middle of the post-sexual revolutionary period. We're now free to discuss sex openly. Let's take advantage of the opportunity and consider to what degree we can integrate our sexuality and our spirituality.

✠ The Christian church today and sexuality

Now, having pointed out that we are in a sexually liberated age where an open discussion of issues of sexuality is acceptable, I should point out to my embarrassment that there has been a distinct lag between what the church says it believes and what it practises.

It's time for the church to resolve its own struggle to integrate sexuality and spirituality. And surely now the time is right. Both sexuality *and* spirituality have come out of the closet. The latter is no longer just reserved for the clergy or the initiated. Many people are actively exploring a spiritual dimension to their lives.

They are yearning for a more down-to-earth spirituality and a wholesome sexuality that can contribute to human growth and integration. I think many people have cottoned on to the fact that their sexuality and their spirituality are not mutually exclusive aspects of their human nature.

Many people can see that when they are sexually damaged in one form or another, this manifests itself spiritually. Those who have been abused sexually usually have great difficulty in making significant relational connections with others in the future. Connection damage — a distinctly spiritual problem — results from sexual relations with the wrong people, or too many people. Never underestimate the degree to which a body that has been damaged by abuse will express the scarring in spiritual ways.

Nevertheless, in her book *I Am My Body*, Elisabeth Moltmann-Wendel suggests that we still speak about ourselves in outdated terms. Our predominant experience is that we *have* a body, with which we work, eat, dance, sleep, relax, make love. She says that sometimes when we are sick, tired or in pain, our perception changes: then we experience that we *are* our bodies.

Certainly, the same could be said when we experience sensations of great bodily pleasure. It seems to me to be a very important observation. At times of extreme sensation, we become one with our bodies, we recognise the strong connection between our body and our being. Normally, during the mundane experience of everyday life, that awareness is lost.

Moltmann-Wendel reckons that the church has been

inconsistent in this regard. While showing remarkable care for sick bodies, it has shown hostility to sexual behaviour. She claims that while the healing of the whole person of both men and women lay at the heart of the Jesus movement, the church has been frightened of and negative about women's bodies in particular. It's time we were much more concerned with the whole person again. In many respects, the call by a theologian like Moltmann-Wendel is a cry to return to the integrated and holistic approach of Jesus himself.

Conceptualising sexuality in its fullest reality should include spirituality and vice versa. I am my sexuality and my spirituality. These are not two warring parties, desperately seeking to have control of me. I am not two persons. I am not a body in opposition to my spirit. I am a spirit as well as a body and, for me to live well, I must be spiritually well.

This is a truth often lost on many people. It is not enough that I eat well, sleep well, laugh well and get plenty of orgasms (though it's a good start). For me to be fully human, I need to feel a connection with the cosmic, the sacred, the mysterious, the transcendent — whatever is 'out there'. To deny the spiritual while developing the sexual (a common mistake) or to work on the spiritual at the expense of your sexuality (a less common mistake these days) is to believe falsely that the spiritual and the sexual operate in different realms.

✠ What spirituality is

We need some clearer definitions. Spirituality, unlike religion, is not primarily a set of beliefs or doctrines, a collection of prayers or a series of rituals. Spirituality is above all a way of seeing. Our spirituality is the resource we have for making sense of our world. It is our particular way of looking at the world. It is different to 'knowing', though only slightly different. Knowing, according to the early seventeenth-century philosopher, Rene Descartes, is the process we engage in for perceiving, analysing and predicting the environment around us.

In many respects, it involves the separation of the individual from 'the world out there', as the individual watches his/her world, begins to make connections between events, predicts future conditions and behaves accordingly. In the late eighteenth century, Immanuel Kant really reinforced this view that 'knowing' was something that a person did confined to his/herself and the contents of his/her consciousness. Spirituality includes knowing, but there's more.

Our spirituality includes what we observe of the world 'out there', but never treats it as being 'out there' at all. Rather, our spirituality is the way humans *connect* with their worlds. It is the stuff of humankind that gives us the energy to interact and be involved in our environment. Knowledge can tell us things about our world, but our spirituality drives us to go forth and be intrinsically connected to that world. Our spirituality could be termed 'our energy for connection'. A deeply spiritual person is one who knows their world and who relates all the elements to each other, not simply as pieces side by side, but as parts of a whole.

But bear in mind that the spiritual person is not

simply making mental notes of random occurrences. He or she is assembling pieces of the pattern, seeing how the patterns relate to each other, as well as distinguishing one part of the pattern to another so that he or she can understand the interrelationship of the parts of the pattern to the whole. This whole includes the knowable and the unknowable — God, mystery, grace, wonder, surprise, serendipity and such like.

If you and I both entered the children's ward of a major hospital, we might possibly make sense of what we see in slightly different ways. I might say to myself, 'What a chaotic, haphazard, frightening world it is we live in. That innocent young children should be victim to such disease or misfortune is a reminder to me that the world is an unfriendly place and for any happiness I can find I should be very grateful. I will vow never to love someone too deeply or risk pain too readily because the chances are I will be deeply hurt for my trouble.'

But you might observe the sight of tiny children suffering and come to the very opposite conclusion. You might think that *because* we are so outraged by innocent suffering, it is not the norm. Rather, it is a reminder that the world for the most part really is a friendly place where we need to love as freely and risk as much as possible to make it even better. The same stimulus can set off different connections in our 'way of seeing the world'. Our spirituality will impact our relationships, our self-image, our values and our choices. The degree to which we can love and risk are directly related to the way we perceive our world.

✠ The link between spirituality and sexuality

From this, it can be seen that there is a very powerful link between our sexuality and our spirituality. Our sexuality is about how we see ourselves in many respects. It is about our gender, about our relationships, about our values and choices. Our sexuality could be called our way of seeing ourselves.

When our sexuality is wounded, it affects the way we see ourself *and* the way we see our world. A person who has been sexually abused in one dreadful form or another will make spiritual connections about their world. They will make determinations about the value of trust in this world or the availabilty of security — or whether the world is a friendly or unfriendly place. On the other hand, when one's sexuality is being expressed, one's view of the world changes.

Have you ever noticed how people who've recently fallen in love see the wonder and majesty in every full moon, the beauty in every spring flower, the twinkle of every star? They believe the world to be a safe, secure, ordered place.

Remember that spirituality is also the response of the whole person — body, mind, spirit, relationships — to the Unknown, to a perceived presence of the holy in the here and now. It is the yearning of every spirit to unite with the ultimate Spirit.

Our sexuality is intrinsically linked to this agenda, but it calls our bodies more explicitly along for the ride. As I mentioned in the previous chapter, a view of sexuality that embraces all of life rather than just as a bodily function (one of the grossest mistakes of the twentieth century) is far more likely to effectively form a foundation for the growth of a human wholeness. It's clear to me that the question of reconciling sexuality and spirituality is the question of achieving human integration or wholeness. It involves having realistic and workable models for femininity and masculinity, but more. Much more.

Since body, psyche and spirit are not separable parts, but rather indistinguishable factors in the human, human wholeness inevitably involves all three. They are different perspectives of the same phenomenon. The spiritual pursuit of truth and value in honesty and love doesn't occur successfully unless it is supported and sustained in a healthy, satisfying, responsive, sensitive and feeling-filled body. There is clear evidence that the quality of the orgasmic experience is highly dependent on the quality of the relationship between the lovers.

The fallacy of modern film makers and television programmers is the assumption that sex between strangers or acquaintances can be good sex every time. Pleasurable, expansive, gratifying sexual experience doesn't really happen unless it is shared in the context of love and honesty. If experienced in commitment and openness, sexual excitement can open us to deeper realities and spiritual dimensions.

Psychiatrist Scott Peck makes much of this connection between sexual pleasure and spirituality. He points out that the French have traditionally referred to orgasm as *le petite mort*, 'the little death'. He says, 'At that brief peak point of little death, we forget who and where we are. And in a very real sense, I think, this is because we have left this earth and entered God's country.'[1]

Sylvia Chavez-Garcia, in an article, *Sexuality and Spirituality: Friends not Foes*, makes much the same point:

> *First, bodily stimulation and sexual excitement have a healing effect as they result in relaxation, calming of the body and release of tension. Further, the intense experience of orgasm temporarily ruptures the world of ideas in which we generally live. . . It opens us to the raw data of experience. . . and so allows the possibility of a new way of seeing and thinking about things.*[2]

Now, it should be noted that sexual gratification for the sake of personal spiritual growth alone is selfish and unintegrated. But Chavez-Garcia is speaking in the context of a committed, loving relationship. Remember that commitment and honesty are means of personal integration also. But Chavez-Garcia recognises this: 'When a couple faces life together in honesty and love, supported by sexual intimacy, then the path of daily life becomes the path to spiritual perfection.'[3]

This is not to suggest that a perfect marriage guarantees spiritual wholeness. What she is saying is that if a couple were to be sexually gratified, both physically and emotionally, they must be growing spiritually, also.

This has been my experience as a minister of religion. Oftentimes, newlywed couples would come to my church with a heightened desire for spiritual growth. Many ministers recognise that as a couple embarks upon marriage, they are keenly open to spiritual truth.

Likewise, I have found another phenomenon that

new mothers will drop into church after giving birth. They come with their brand new babies to church to attend services, often without their partners. I believe these are women who have, through the experience of childbirth, connected strongly with their sexual selves and this has opened to them the possibility of spiritual growth. Like all new discoveries, some continue to grow spiritually and others stop appearing after a few weeks.

Scott Peck suggests the reverse is also true. Just as a strong awareness of our sexual selves draws us towards spiritual growth, because it draws us out of ourselves to others, to love, to vulnerability; so do deeply spiritual experiences open us to greater possibilities sexually. He says:

> About a dozen years ago, after many months of working with a rigid, frigid woman in her mid-thirties, I had the opportunity to witness her undergo a sudden and quite profound Christian conversion. And within three weeks of that conversion, she became orgasmic for the first time. Could the timing have been accidental? I doubt it.[4]

It's clear that the sexual and spiritual parts of our personality (if they can accurately be described as 'parts') are so closely interrelated that it's impossible to arouse the one without arousing the other. Peck goes on to point out that he has a friend, a priest, who actually uses this phenomenon as a yardstick of conversion. He believes that if a conversion occurs in a previously sexually repressed person and is not accompanied by some degree of sexual awakening, then he doubts the depth of the conversion!

This does not mean that deeply spiritual people are wandering around looking for new sexual experiences like that randy old monk, Rasputin. It does mean that deeply spiritual people have their senses heightened. Their radar is up. They are looking for stimulation. There is a fresh desire to re-encounter their worlds, to experience beauty, light, love, wonder.

For those who are unmarried, this may never manifest itself as a full-blown sexual relationship with another person. But it will be manifest by a heightened level of intimacy with others, of vulnerability, of openness and inclusivity. For married people, it may well be experienced between the sheets with their spouse, but I would hope that's not only where it is manifest.

I've always enjoyed the television series called *Northern Exposure*. It concerns the eccentric, quirky residents of the small Alaskan town of Cicely. And the character to whom I feel most drawn is that of the town's disc jockey-cum-spiritual guru, Chris Stevens.

Chris, obviously a deeply spiritual man to begin with, is a former prisoner whose life had more or less fallen apart when he came to Cicely to start afresh. As the series has unfolded, viewers have been observers to his spiritual awakening and his deep personal growth. We are now used to Chris philosophising or theologising between playing tracks on his breakfast show. He regularly quotes St Augustine, Theresa of Avila, Miester Ekhardt, Thomas Merton and others.

In one of my very favourite episodes, Chris leaves Cicely for a spiritual retreat at a Catholic monastery. He is already deeply impressed with the vows of chastity and poverty made by monks he has read about and desires nothing more than to learn from this order the secret of how to become dead to the world. He actually looks forward to wearing cassocks and hair shirts, to eating gruel and sleeping on boards, to the back-breaking labour and the hours of spiritual duties. He wants nothing more than to be able to deny his need for worldly pleasure and leave this temporal plane for a higher spiritual existence.

On his first day at the monastery, he is assigned to tend the beehives where the monks collect honey for sale. There, he meets the enigmatic Brother Simon who, he is told, has taken a vow of silence. In fact, Brother Simon has vowed to withdraw completely from this world. Simon eats alone, works in silence and eschews any contact with other people. He always wears his hood over his face or his beekeeper's gauze mask when working.

Though never having heard his voice or seen his face, Chris naturally finds this extremely alluring. Simon is fulfilling all of Chris' personal desires. Chris, who viewers will know can't shut up for a second, is overwhelmed by the spirituality of one who can choose to be silent as an exercise of religious devotion.

So far this mightn't seem too unusual, but there's a scene almost halfway through this episode that takes your breath away. As he labours with the beehives with Brother Simon, Chris suddenly reaches out to the monk, embraces him passionately and kisses him longingly through the wire gauze face mask he is wearing. We then see Chris sit up in bed heaving for breath. It was only a dream. But it begins a series of erotic dreams Chris then has about the silent, faceless Brother Simon, something he cannot understand because he has always been strongly heterosexual.

Chris confesses these dreams to the Abbott who tells him he must confess them to Simon. In fact, even while attempting to make his confession to Simon later that day, he inadvertently expresses strong sexual desire for the monk.

Well, in a quirky (and, I think, unnecessary) ending, Brother Simon pulls back his hood only to reveal that he is really a she, thereby setting Chris and the issue of his sexual orientation at ease.

The reason I like this episode so much is that it makes an attempt to connect Chris' burgeoning spirituality with a related heightened sexual awareness. Not many popular TV programs attempt to deal with such deep issues. Chris discovered on his retreat what we should have all known for centuries: sexuality and spirituality are closely linked. Don't arouse one if you're not prepared to allow the other to develop as well.

And just as a small note of caution, single people oughtn't to be afraid of this development in their sexuality, but they should be careful to be responsible in its expression. There are many ways to express our sexuality to another without genital stimulation. And neither should we ever assume that just because a spiritual person is married, their avenue for sexual expression is clear cut. How many great religious leaders have fallen into sexual misconduct? Do you think that one of the reasons why this is the case is the fact that, as these people developed spiritually, they also became more sexually aware? All the more reason for us to be developing sexually and spiritually in mature, sensible, responsible ways long before we become leaders (if that's our thing!).

✠ Richard Neibuhr and the dynamic relationship between sexuality and spirituality

So, how can we be more explicit about the relationship between my sexuality and my spirituality? We do need a theological framework for making sense of the dynamic relationship between them. I think it can be provided by the American theologian, Richard Niebuhr.

For those who know some theology, Niebuhr might seem like the most unlikely source for helping to integrate sexuality and spirituality. Richard Niebuhr is best noted for his work on religion and culture. But two contemporary theological teachers have alerted me to his value in this regard. Joan Timmerman, in *Sexuality and Spiritual Growth* and Geoffrey Wainwright, in *The Study of Spirituality*, have both borrowed heavily from Niebuhr in their discussions on this topic.

Richard Niebuhr spoke of four models for the way religion, specifically Christianity, interacts with culture. Both Wainwright and Timmerman (separately) have used these models for discussing the way sexuality and spirituality should interact.

1. *Niebuhr's first model is typified as being Christ-against-culture.* He reckoned that many religious people see culture as being hopelessly corrupt and that our only

choice is an absolute either-or, all-or-nothing decision to abandon the one for the other. The world is seen as hostile to the cause of God.

This school of thought sees spirituality (Christ) and sexuality (culture) as separated by a gulf that can never be bridged. The early monastaries and hermitages were founded on this basis. The monastic movement saw Christ and culture in direct conflict. One had to be denied for the other to be fully released. Of course, the early monks and nuns and hermits also saw sexuality as being in conflict with spirituality, as we noted earlier.

This model, though popular throughout Christian history, is still surfacing regularly around the world today. Those who condemn the 'evils of the world' and demand a withdrawal from contemporary culture are as varied as the fundamentalist Christian denominations to sects like the Branch Davidians in Waco, Texas. It is an approach that is deficient in several ways.

First, it considers sexuality and spirituality as mutually exclusive — and I think we can see that they're not.

Second, this model assumes that God's love is thought to be discontinuous with human love — that divine and human love cannot overlap. But this is not an assumption that Christ ever made.

And third, it has never been adequately demonstrated that by isolating ourselves, we can guarantee faithfulness and purity. In fact, Christ himself clearly modelled a life of connection with others, not isolation. We simply can't go back to trying to isolate our sexuality from our spirituality, as if we were ever called to do so in the first place.

2. *Niebuhr's second model is Christ-as-culture.* It is a pendulum swing to the other extreme. If you thought the first view is too pessimistic about culture (or sexuality), this perspective is decidedly — and dangerously — optimistic about them. In fact, it collapses the spiritual into the cultural. In this model, there is no need for faith and no hope of transformation. American Christianity has been accused of adopting this stance, where to be a good citizen is to be a good Christian and vice versa. The fundamentalist theocracies of the Middle East are another case in point.

The other danger of this approach is what has been called the descent into hedonism. This is the mistaken belief that complete fulfilment can come through the pursuit of pleasure. It is as though we have re-adopted the primitive, pagan religious system that believed spiritual purity was appropriated *through* physical gratification. It descends into selfishness and the abuse of relationships as we single-mindedly pursue physical pleasures to the exclusion of others.

Good religious outlooks bring people together. This approach does not. This descent naturally leads to the paradox of hedonism — the simple fact that pleasure can never satisfy completely.

When related to the sexuality-spirituality issue, the Christ-as-culture model also falls short. Whereas the Christ-against-culture model finds them mutually exclusive, this model identifies them uncritically. The unchallenged prevailing culture dictates sexual ethics. Masculine domination might, for example, be considered the norm, but this doesn't in any way reflect the concerns of Christ.

Likewise, a self-centred, destructive commitment to pursue sexual gratification will alienate a person from those he uses in the process. It might be the norm — in fact, we currently have a phenomenon called 'sex-addiction' being spoken of in the tabloid press — but it's not an indication of a healthy, integrated human being. Confrontation with culture is rare and, normally, an endorsement of the *status quo* is strongly implied.

3. *Niebuhr's third model is Christ-above-culture.* This belief views the affairs of humans to be neatly divided into sacred and secular compartments, where rarely the twain shall meet. It emphasises positive elements in human nature, but recognises that even they need to be purified. The sacred is *above* the secular, seeking to invade, to purify the secular.

A lot of the co-dependency support groups which rely on a 'power greater than yourself' to save the person from the worst possibilities fit into this category. Most forms of New Age spirituality emphasise this model wherein the crystal, the forces of nature or psychic powers are the sources of power outside the individual. This model has some things to commend it, but basically it insists on the superiority of the spiritual, though it would allow a 'purified' sex life as compatible with it.

4. *Niebuhr's fourth model is Christ-the-transformer-of-culture.* It is founded clearly on two essential Christian doctrines: creation and incarnation. This means that God not only created this planet and everything on it, but is involved in the re-creative process of history. Further, it states that God has actively entered into human affairs by incarnating himself as a human and engaging in culture.

This isn't to say that God has a completely uncritical view of culture (as in the Christ-as-culture model). Conversion and rebirth are needed not to replace the sacred with the secular, but to open the individual to being the incarnation of God in this world as well. When God dwells within the individual, together they become part of the process of transforming dominant cultural norms that don't concur with the agenda of God.

I believe that a healthy integration of spirituality and sexuality can best be achieved through this model. It's a superior model because it sees all love as continuous with God's love and sexual life as transformative of all life. It includes openness to reality in all its dimensions. It affirms the interconnectedness of human living.

It also demands that we abandon the compartmentalised approaches of the other models. Spirituality doesn't just deal with the 'top half' of reality . It deals with the whole of reality as it is, without artificially imposed compartments. Jesus lived a life where he was neither in conflict with culture, nor sold out to dominant cultural norms. But neither was he above culture, drawing his disciples gradually into the 'top half' of reality. He embodied God's presence in this world, mingling and entwining current realities and forcing new, more righteous formulations. This is called the incarnation.

The same, I believe, should be said of integrating

sexuality and spirituality. Neither one is 'better' or 'above' the other. They are different facets of the same thing. And, as such, they ought to be mingled together, each one informing the other, each one drawing the most out of the other. To set them in conflict, or to have one ignore the other, is inhuman.

✠ **The source of our understanding of sexuality**
What we need is a more fully considered approach to sexuality. We need better, more workable paradigms for understanding masculinity and femininity, and we need the resources to embrace healthy sexual and spiritual experiences, recognising the dependence of the one upon the other.

We have briefly tracked the issues and raised several questions. But we need a starting point. We need an anchor to ground this discussion (or a chandelier to swing from!). I want to suggest that the best place to start is God.

I know I've alluded to this several times already. You might say I've threatened this several times. But if we're to recognise seriously the integration of spirit and body, we need to start at the source. We need to begin with God.

I believe there is a genuine sexual element in the relationship between human beings and God. Many theologians, including the great Karl Barth, suggest that human sexuality reflects the differentiation of persons within the godhead and God's intimately relational nature. The idea follows that, since God created us in his own image, that is (according to Barth) 'in correspondence to his own being and essence', that our sexual natures reflect the nature of God. It stands to reason that if we are spiritual beings because he is Spirit, then we must be sexual beings because he is sexual.

This might resemble anthropomorphism (imagining God in human terms), but the deepest means we have truly to understand God is through a projection onto him of the very best of our human nature. In this respect, God is *humane*. He represents humanity at its best. We can learn about ourselves, including our sexual selves, by looking at our best formulations for God.

I must be explicit in what I'm saying here. I don't mean that God is sexual in the sense that he is either male or female. Neither male nor female sexuality can be adequately attributed to God. I mean that the 'movements' usually associated with masculinity and femininity are the movements of God. I mean that the core goals, the ultimate meanings, the means of connection and the energy of bonding attributed to masculinity and femininity can equally be attributed to God.

As theologian, Mary Hayter, says in her book *The New Eve In Christ*, when speaking about the masculine and feminine language used in the Bible to refer to God:

> *The masculine terminology does not denote a male deity; the female terminology does not denote a female deity; nor does the mixture of masculine and feminine terminology denote an androgynous God/ess. Rather, the indications are that the God of the Bible uniquely incorporates and trancends all sexuality.*[5]

In effect our sexuality, fashioned by God, reminds us

of our creator. It is a basic human hunger that sends us news from a country we have not visited. It sends us signals of the way in which God interacts with the universe.

The fact is, many of us are poor stewards of our own sexuality. We need some more objective information for understanding this God who is hinted at through our sexuality. And the place to find that information is in the ancient stories we have been told about God since the beginning. If we are made to find our ultimate satisfaction in him, what then is he really like?

4

THE PARADOX OF GOD

What divine mystery is like

The reason why the element of paradox comes into all religious thought and statement is because God cannot be comprehended in any human words or in any of the categories of our finite thought.

D.M. Baillie

God is the Being. . . that may properly only be addressed, not expressed.

Martin Buber

GARRISON KEILLOR, THE MUCH-LOVED American humorist, once said: 'To know and to serve God, of course, is why we're here, a clear truth that, like the nose on your face, is near at hand and easily discernible, but can make you dizzy if you try to focus on it hard.' How true! Here, so neatly put, is the paradox associated with trying to know God. He is both near at hand and hard to focus on. He is both readily available and mysteriously unknowable. He is close and yet far. He is enticing and yet frightening. He is gentle and yet harsh. He, like all truth, is best expressed paradoxically.

When we claim that God is sexual as we are sexual, we necessarily must claim him to have both feminine and masculine traits. By doing so, we are making what seems like a contradictory statement. How can he be both? Surely God must be one or the other — preferably the former, say many people. But the simple fact of the matter is that God clearly demonstrates traits that are usually associated with femininity as much as those associated with masculinity. This is part of the great paradoxical nature of God.

We as humans, made in the likeness of God, share in this paradox. Carl Jung has said that within the collective consciousness of all human beings there resides personality traits usually considered to be masculine and feminine, and that we are conditioned socially to suppress the one or the other, depending upon our gender.

In other words, while men are encouraged to exhibit traits usually perceived to be masculine (assertiveness, competitiveness, logic, aggression), they have the potential to unleash traits hidden in their unconscious that are usually considered feminine (nurturing, intuition, etc.) and vice versa.

It stands to reason that since we are reflections of the God who made us, he too exhibits characteristics that are both masculine and feminine. Sadly, however, the church has traditionally suppressed the latter. Therefore, quite often, only God's masculine appeal has held sway. We have been presented with a male God and heard language that describes him as competitive, aggressive, all-knowing, all-powerful, desiring to have, penetrate, own, love us. I have no objection to this, since this aspect of God is celebrated in the Bible very often. But surely it's not the whole story.

Would it be that if we presented the equally impressive, but feminine traits of birthing, nurturing, fostering, comforting, we could encounter a God who desires to enfold us as much as to enter us? The feminine side of God could prove as alluring as has his masculine side. It would allow God to entice us all, irrespective of gender.

As surely as wholeness comes when human beings choose to integrate the conscious and unconscious elements of our psyche, so would we encounter the whole of God if we allowed both the divine feminine and masculine traits to be unleashed. It's true of men and women. Why wouldn't it be true of God in whose image we were created?

✠ The power and value of paradox

But first, we need to understand this idea of the paradoxical nature of God. It has been said that virtually all basic truth is paradoxical. In fact, there's an old joke about the famous professor who was asked by one of his students: 'Is it correct you believe that at the core of all reality there is a paradox?' The professor responded, 'Well, yes and no.' To express a truth through a paradox is to set up opposite ideas in tension with each other and to be prepared to accept that the mysterious nature of that truth is found in the dynamic energy in each of them forcing the other away. In fact, there is enormous power in setting apparently contradictory truths against each other in order to reveal an even greater insight.

I think it can be safely said that in order to understand Christianity we need to be able to appreciate the power of paradox. Perhaps a dictionary-style definition will do the trick. A paradox is a statement or proposition that seems self-contradictory or even absurd and yet can be demonstrated as expressing a truth. And the Bible is full of them. God is considered mysterious and yet knowable; Jesus is both human and divine; the first are considered last and the last first; human nature is described as being made in God's image and yet sinful and ungodly. In fact, the list goes on and on: those who wish to find life must first lose it; to follow God involves both individual freedom and corporate responsibility. Paradox is the underlying motif in all biblical teaching.

The reason for looking at paradox is not to explode any reliance on rational thought or logical progression, but to be brutally honest about the basic truths of the universe. They are rarely quite so easy to pin down. In this regard, Christianity is eminently realistic.

To understand paradox, one must be prepared to embrace both poles or opposites and *synthesise* them in a balanced kind of way. By so doing, we create a new level of depth. In fact, this process opens our minds to new possibilities and broadens our current ways of thinking. But note that I used the term synthesise, not compromise. When we compromise, we lose part of each of the opposite poles in an attempt to accommodate both. The synthesis embraces both truths equally and at the same time.

Another related term is 'synergy' — the combination of two things working together which exceeds the sum of the individual parts. Said the Danish philosopher, Søren Kierkegaard: 'The paradox is the source of the thinker's passion, and the thinker without a paradox is like a lover without feeling: a paltry mediocrity.'[1]

For example, the idea that God is both masculine and feminine seems absurd. But so does the idea that God is both very near and yet very hard to see. It's a nonsense. Either he's near or he's not. Either you can see him or you can't. But those of us who have encountered the presence of God know that both statements are true. There are times when he seems as obvious as the nose on your face. But try to examine the nose on your face for very long and you end up cross-eyed.

I think Garrison Keillor knows what he's talking about. And so you'll discover, as you read the Bible, many seemingly contradictory ideas about God littered throughout various sections of the ancient material.

In some cases, God seems near and intimate and closely aligned with his people. At other times, he seems mysterious and terrible and deposited upon high. To embrace paradox is to be prepared to admit that both these opposites can be true if we recognise that the energy that is released by the tension between them forms some of the 'stuff' of God.

When you place the north ends of two magnets next to each other, they are repulsed. One of them is forced away from the other. But when you hold them in tension and feel the power, the energy, the dynamism of their repulsion, you sense the real marvel of magnetic fields. Sensing that invisible and yet seemingly tangible force called electricity between the two poles is almost magical. The trick is in holding them at just the right distance with just the right force to feel the energy. That's also the trick to embracing Christian theology.

Unfortunately, a lot of Christian thinkers are trying to propositionalise Christianity. By the term 'propositionalise' I mean the process of seeking to capture truth within a series of statements that, when affirmed, define the body of truth that determines one as a 'believer' or not. That makes it so simple and straightforward, doesn't it? Yet there is a twinge of uncertainty when confronted with this approach to Christian belief. Everything is cut and dried. If you agree with the first propositional statement, you move on to the second and so forth until, by the end of it, if you've understood and affirmed all the steps, you've understood Christianity.

Please don't ever believe it's that simple. I'm certainly not implying you need a PhD in order to figure out what Christianity is about. But you do need a commitment to reality and an unswerving desire to find a faith that is robust enough to deal with the unsettling and haphazard nature of life. Propositions won't always hold true in every situation. But paradoxical truth can. Therapist John Bradshaw refers to propositionalising as 'totalistic thinking', a simplistic righteousness that denies the complexity and struggle that comes with seeking truth. He says: 'Reducing the mystery of God to simplistic formulas is grandiose and downright idolatrous. Such reduction destroys the soul itself'.[2]

When I was doing my undergraduate degree in theology, I remember attending a class during which the lecturer wanted us to define God. And so we workshopped on this task. We broke into groups and determined which features of God's character ought to be in any such definition and what aspects of his way of relating to human beings would be helpful in this statement.

Then all the groups came back together and we fed information to the lecturer who scrawled our definitive statement on the old blackboard at the front of the room. We all tussled and argued about whether this line ought to go at the end or the middle. We to-ed and fro-ed over including this aspect or excluding that, until by the end of the two-hour session we had a pretty hefty propositional statement that nearly filled the whole board. 'There,' declared the teacher, pointing to the dusty, chalk-written definition. 'There is God. Copy him down and you can go.'

There was something terribly dissatisfying about copying God down onto my pad of lecture notes and stuffing him in my satchel before heading off to the common room for coffee. In fact, I think that was the effect my theology lecturer had in mind when he initiated the exercise.

The fact of the matter is that propositional statements don't always do the trick. Here's an example. Suppose I made the following statement: 'The sea is a friendly place.' Most people would be able to agree that, yes, the sea is a friendly place. You might recall days spent paddling in rock pools by the water's edge. Images of summer holidays would spring to mind — frolicking in the waves, walking along the beach with your first love, learning to ride a board, bodysurfing, swimming out beyond the sets, feeling the invigorating salt water on your face. Yes, the sea is a friendly place!

But what if I had said gravely, 'The sea is an unfriendly place'? Most people would affirm that, indeed, the sea is an unfriendly place. You could recall the panic of being chundered in a dumping shore break and being turned over and over and wondering whether you'd ever reach the surface. Some would have had the frightening experience of being caught in a rip or being swept off the rocks at a beach headland. Some may have been caught in a squall while sailing up or down the coast. To feel the awesome and uncontrollable power of the ocean is a fearful thing. We would agree that the sea is deep beyond imagining and black as pitch. The sheer size and strength of the sea is an unsettling thing.

Yes, the sea is an unfriendly place!

You see, both statements are true. They are clearly demonstrable. An entity as large and as complex as the sea cannot be described so tritely by one definitive statement. Those who have waded into the shallows at Monkey Mia in Western Australia and hand fed dolphins in the crystal clear, aqua blue ocean will have been astounded by the friendliness of the sea. And anyone who saw *Jaws* in a darkened cinema years ago didn't venture into the water past their knees the next time they made it to the beach.

Of course, anyone who has discovered a small deserted beach on their travels will have known the feeling of 'owning' the sea. Being on a small stretch of sand, cocooned by imposing headlands, hearing the lullaby of the surf lapping at the shore, makes you feel like you're 'home'. But if you've ever flown over the ocean and experienced endless blue water to every horizon you know what it's like to be overwhelmed by its vastness.

Being an Australian, I relate to the paradoxical nature of the sea very clearly. Though we live on this huge island, we cling steadfastly to the sea, bunching together around the rim of the red continent, relating to the sea as both friend and foe, both drawn to it and repulsed by it.

I think the sea is a telling illustration of what God is like. Just as the sea is both friendly and unfriendly, playful and terrifying, close at hand and far away, comforting and unsettling, so is the God of the Bible. He cannot ever be entirely summed up by propositional theological statements. He is not so simple as some would make out. Like the deep dark ocean, he is hard to encounter, a respecter of no man. Like the gentle lapping of the surf on the sand, he is welcoming and near at hand.

Of course, this analogy can't be pressed too far. The sea isn't a personal entity. It has no basic character or will, as such. God, on the other hand, is an entirely personal being with a will and with certain personality traits. The sea is a great reflector of God's closeness and his mystery.

Perhaps, however, it is even more helpful to use the more personal concept of *parent* to further illustrate the paradox of God. If I was to suggest to you that God is the most exquisitely divine *father* imaginable, what might spring to mind? Strength? Dependability? Fair discipline? A good provider? Measured? Sincere? Honest?

But alternatively, what if we make the suggestion that God is the image of the perfect *mother*? What impressions might we have of such a suggestion? Loving? Tender? Gentle? Comforting? Intuitive? Loyal? Are these reasonable impressions of God? I think so. It would certainly seem that God embodies the best aspects of what it is to be both mother and father.

But what happens when these aspects seem to be in tension? The discipliner and the comforter are very different roles. Can they be embodied in the same person? The way the Bible describes God indicates they can be. The biblical pictures of God embrace the tension of paradox with a great degree of confidence and resilience.

The mystery of understanding God involves the same trick as holding the magnets in tension. It calls for us to believe at the same time and equally that God is both near and far away, both feminine and masculine.

It's quite a trick, isn't it? But surely it's no more difficult for us than embracing the mystery of the sea. Of course, there are times when the sea's closeness is more apparent to us than its awesomeness and vice versa.

You'll find the same with God. At times his masculinity will prove very seductive to you and, at other times, his femininity.

✠ The paradox of God's transcendence and immanence

However, before we explore the masculine and feminine aspects to God's character, it will be important to look more closely at the paradox of God in traditional theology. I think you'll find hints in the traditional understandings of God's character that will allow us to more fully appreciate the seductive nature of his dealings with us as sexual beings. Traditional theology is not bad. It very adequately describes a good deal about God, but not all there is to know about him. If we go back to basics and rediscover what the Christian church understands about God, you'll discover that an acceptance of the masculinity and femininity of God will follow quite naturally.

In order for us to rediscover these long held understandings about God, we need to re-aquaint ourselves with the stories that have been told about God since the earliest days of civilisation. It's my view that we humans, in our quest to know God, have sought to do so through the powerful tool called 'the story'. Sadly, in our so-called sophisticated culture today, we think of stories as being only for little children. But the story is, in fact, one of the basic building blocks of what we call our corporate wisdom.

Robert Bly in his book about men, *Iron John*, and Clarissa Pinkola Estes in her book on women, *Women Who Run With The Wolves*, have both sought to discover clues to understanding masculinity and femininity through exhaustive studies of ancient stories. Robert Bly explains it this way:

> *The knowledge of how to build a nest in a bare tree, how to fly to the wintering place, how to perform the mating dance ---- all of this information is stored in the reservoirs of the bird's instinctual brain. But human beings, sensing how much flexibility they might need in meeting new situations, decided to store this sort of knowledge outside the instinctual system; they stored it in stories.*[3]

There are stories, both factual and fictional, that have

been told by the Christian community — and the Hebrew community before it — that are the storehouses, the reservoirs in which our ways of responding to God, understanding him and our relationship with him have been kept. Our concern here is to re-examine those stories for clues to the paradoxical nature of God.

Traditionally, the church has understood the paradoxical nature of God to be expressed in his *transcendence* and his *immanence*. 'Transcendence' is the term employed to describe God's mystery, his distance from us, his 'bigness', his majesty and glory. In many respects, this term hints at many of the characteristics of God that we consider to be masculine: his competitiveness with other gods; his wrath; his rightness in all situations; his aloofness.

On the other hand, and held in tension with his transcendence, is the idea of immanence. This term indicates God's closeness to his people. Again, this echoes many of the ideas we have of femininity: intimacy, loyalty, mercy and favour. These terms aren't in and of themselves masculine or feminine terms, but they do contain traces of the distinctions we draw between the two.

They are not specifically religious words. You won't find them in the Bible stories we will examine at all. 'Transcending' refers to someone or something going beyond its normal limits or confines. We could say the volume of the seas transcends human imagining. That is, it is outside the realm of human comprehension. But when we refer to the transcendence of God, we are meaning the way he goes beyond the normal limits of the material universe (and the realm of human comprehension, for that matter). We're talking about his vastness.

The term 'immanence' is an ordinary word, describing something that is within, something that is inherent or indwelling. When applied to God it means his 'closeness'. Theologian Louis Berkhof, when discussing these two ideas, prefers to use the terms 'transcendence' and 'condescendence' because the latter implies a more active quality on God's part than the passive term 'immanence'. I see his point, but I'll stick with the more traditional idea of God's immanence being the opposite idea to his transcendence. We need to explore these ideas for a while, because to ignore them and to launch into an exploration of God's masculine and feminine sides without this foundational work is theological malpractice. As the Old Testament prophet, Jeremiah says, speaking on behalf of God himself, 'Am I only a God nearby, declares the Lord, and not a God far away?'[4] Indeed, he is both.

The Christian church throughout the centuries has been resolved to believe in *both* God's transcendence *and* immanence equally and at the same time. Says the great Christian theologian, Karl Rahner, 'God himself as the abiding and holy mystery, as the incomprehensible ground of man's transcendent existence, is not only the God of infinite distance, but also wants to be the God of absolute closeness in a true self-communication. . .'[5]

And there it is in a nutshell.

5

THE HOLY, TRANSCENDENT GOD
What divine greatness looks like

> *Our picture of God must resemble more the violence of a sunset painting by Turner than a watery wash by a maiden aunt!*
>
> C.A. Coulson
>
> *It is a terrible thing to fall into the hands of the living God*
>
> Hebrews 10, verse 31

THELOGIANS CAME UP WITH THE TERM 'transcendence', so you won't find it in the Bible. The term employed by the storytellers of the Bible that most clearly describes this aspect of God's character is the word 'holiness'.

✠ The holiness of God

I wouldn't be exaggerating if I said that in the Old Testament in particular, the term 'holiness' overshadows all the other adjectives associated with God. Even in the New Testament, the emphasis only shifts slightly because the writers took the presuppositions of the Old Testament as given.

There are two basic ideas behind the word 'holiness'. The first is separateness, transcendence, uniqueness, *otherness*. It implies that God's greatness sets him apart, distinguishing him as the wholly *Other*. In fact, 'holiness' is the name of the category into which only God fits. It is a central and indispensible understanding of God. The second idea is that of moral perfection, affirming God's stainless, unblemished nature. He is completely whole, pristine, incapable of poor judgment or wrongdoing. Try to imagine the depth and the darkness of the deepest, darkest part of the ocean and even then you've not remotely imagined the depths of God's holiness. Along these lines, Bette Midler sings: 'God is watching us, from a distance.'

How can you describe the holiness of God? I don't really think we can, since holiness is the very thing that sets God apart from us and our world. If we could capture it with words, it would lose its magic, its meaning. Jurgen Moltmann once said quite wisely: 'We do better to adore the mysteries of deity than to explain them.' To some degree we will be exploring the uninhabitable, seeking to know the unknowable.

Actually, there are a good many people who devote their entire lives to thinking about God, who live their lives in a pious devotion to God and the Bible and yet who are really nowhere near knowing or understanding God. You see, it's virtually impossible to grasp the otherness of God with our tiny minds.

The Christian mystic, Joel S. Goldsmith, has pointed

out that the otherness (holiness) of God can only be expressed in the phrase 'God is':

> Mainomides, the Hebrew mystic, wrote that when you say, 'God is good, God is all power, God is all mighty, God is great', you are really only saying 'God is'. The great Catholic mystic Julian of Norwich, who wrote The Cloud of Unknowing, said that when you say 'God is love, or God is divine love, God is omniscience', you are only saying 'God is'.[1]

God's transcendent holiness is too enormous, too deep ever to be truly limited to the confines of human language. But language is all we've got in this case. So as long as we bear in mind the inadequacy of this endeavour, I still think this exercise has some considerable value.

✠ Aspects of God's holiness

We have needed some idea of who God is and what it means for him to be holy. Surely, there are some concepts we might use on which to hang this remarkable aspect of God's nature. Another theologian, James Montgomery Boice, an American, has sought to come up with just those concepts.[2] He suggests that holiness as presented in the Bible's stories has at least four discernible elements.

❏ The first aspect of God's holiness: majesty

'Majesty' is a word that implies dignity and stateliness, grandeur, sovereignty and power. The term is still used of earthly monarchs like kings and queens. In days when royal rulers were believed to be the worldly representatives of gods (or in some cultures, to be gods themselves), the same attributes of the deities were ascribed to the monarchs. Therefore, the majestic nature of the gods was mimicked by the kings and queens who represented them.

One of the throwbacks of this belief is that we refer to the Queen of England as 'Her Majesty'. It refers to her ascribed position as God's royal representative. Now, we don't believe she is divine or that she has been endowed by God with certain godly characteristics above and beyond the norm. We all know that she is flesh and blood like the rest of us. We are aware that in many ways she is probably just like any other English grandmother. She didn't have to pass some majesty quotient test to become a queen. But we call her 'Majesty' as a courtesy, because her role and the way in which she carries it out have been characterised by grace, dignity and stateliness.

In this regard, the current British monarch fulfils the function of providing us with an inkling of what true majesty looks like. Of course, the majesty of God's holiness is far and away more impressive than Elizabeth R's. As James Boice says: '[It is] supremely of that One who is Monarch over all. Majesty is the dominant element in the visions of God in his glory, seen both in the Old Testament and the New.'[3]

☐ *The second aspect of God's holiness: jealousy*
The second element in the idea of holiness is that of *will*. This refers to the will of a personality. You see,

while I love the analogy of God being like the sea, it needs to be reiterated that the sea has no will; it has no personality. Of course, we can ascribe human characteristics to the sea — like friendliness, for example. But we can't make a case for the sea having any specific will. It is an inanimate object.

There is nothing inanimate about God, however. He, like any personality, has a will. He is capable of volitional and judicious decision-making. Boice makes the interesting point that God's will is primarily expressed in his 'jealousness'.

To be jealous is not a great virtue. So how can jealousy be admired in God? It's important that we understand what's meant when the Bible speaks of God's jealousness.

This idea is probably most explicitly stated in Exodus 20, verse 5: 'I the Lord your God am a jealous God.' Emil Brunner, a Christian thinker of considerable note, argues that this kind of jealousy is not the green-eyed monster known to so many of us. Jealousy in human relationships usually belies a deep sense of insecurity. Not so when God talks about being jealous. It's more like the kind of jealousy that's appropriate within marriage. Just as a married couple should rightfully expect that a third person should not be allowed to enter into the intimacy of their relationship, God rejects any attack on his relationship with humankind.

As a minister, I have frequently been contacted by individuals who are concerned that their partner is becoming infatuated by a third party. Occasionally, they have said something like, 'Well, I guess if so-and-so can meet certain needs that I can't, then it's best for both of us that he/she be happy. If I love him/her, then I should allow a little latitude, shouldn't I?'

'No!' I usually respond. 'It makes no sense to me that in a loving relationship, one person can be forced to subjugate their feelings and allow their partner to blackmail them emotionally into letting them have the occasional fling.'

Well-known medical doctor and family therapist, James Dobson, wrote a book called *Love Must be Tough*. It deals with this very situation in which one member of a partnership is having an affair while the other member feels compelled to turn a blind eye to it all in order to 'keep' the relationship. As if the title doesn't say it all, Dobson coined the phrase 'loving toughness' and he commends the faithful partners to exercise this kind of love. It's the kind of loving that respects self.

In fact, it was Jesus who taught us that we must love others *as much as we love ourselves*. Many people have a dreadful time loving/respecting themselves and therefore allow themselves to be demeaned or humiliated by an uncaring partner. Tough love is self-loving love. It demands respect and dignity for self and refuses to allow another to debase it.

Tough love is not insecure or demanding or immature. It is based on self-respect and dignity. God's tough love is just the same. One cannot be majestic and co-exist in relationships that are demeaning and disrespectful. I recall seeing some news footage of the British royal family at Balmoral during which the Queen sought to make some grandmotherly contact with little Prince

William, who was then about three or four years old. As she bent to speak to him, he stuck out his tongue and blew a raspberry at her and bolted. For a brief minute, the Queen didn't look terribly majestic. In fact, she looked very normal.

However, since God is perfect and his majesty can never be compromised, it is quite simply impossible for him to stop being a king and become a normal grandfather every so often. His holiness predicates his refusal to be treated without the dignity that is due him. His jealousy is really his tough and uncompromising commitment to expect the unswerving devotion of his people.

Usually, we think of jealousy as the emotional response of a weak person. It invariably veils insecurity and fear. For that reason, the word 'jealousy' itself may not be a good one, but I can think of no better replacement — as long as you recognise that in this instance it refers to the tough, unyielding, relentless, demanding, powerful love of a God who will not be trifled with. He will not allow himself to be dismissed lightly — or ignored, for that matter. His very holiness demands that we respond in some kind. This 'jealousy' is probably best defined as *tough love!*

I remember a friend of mine once wrote what he believed to be a fairly radical article on a religious issue, which was accepted by and printed in a very reputable theological journal. He was delighted at being published and anticipated quite a hullabuloo in the church world. I saw him some time later and asked about the reaction his article had illicited. He appeared clearly upset. 'Did you get a rough reception, mate?' I asked.

'No. Worse.' he responded glumly. 'No response at all.'

As much as we dislike a negative reaction, even that is better than no reaction at all. To be ignored or disdained or, at best, just barely tolerated is an even more bitter pill to swallow than to be rejected. In our Australian culture, being rejected is sometimes a form of endearment. I'm not advocating this particular cultural quirk, but let's be frank about it: when you get bagged at the pub, you know you're okay. Being ignored is the greatest humiliation.

God's jealousy has a similar overtone. God's holiness is so great it cannot be dismissed. It urges a response either in its favour or against it. Says James Boice:

> '. . .the holiness of God means that God is not indifferent to how men and women regard him. He does not go his solitary way heedless of their rejection of him. Rather, he wills and acts to see that his glory is recognised.'[4]

☐ *The third aspect of God's holiness: wrath*
The third element that Boice suggests in the idea of holiness is that of *wrath*. And just as I had to redefine the term 'jealousy', so will I need to redefine wrath. Most people think of it as another word for anger, but in the case of God's wrath it's a bit different.

Human anger is an emotional response to certain stimuli. Some anger is justified and appropriate. Some — most — is certainly not. It's right to be angry at injustice, for example, because invariably your anger develops into some kind of proactive response. If some form of injustice incites you to anger, the chances are it will also incite you to action. But when you become angry because the garage door won't open easily or because you are simply not getting what you want, there is no productive value in the anger at all. In fact, there is usually a destructive element present.

God's wrath is not at all like crankiness or impatience. Actually, the chances are that human beings have no notion at all what godly wrath really is, because it is so beyond our experience. Whereas anger is an emotional response, godly wrath seems to be quite unemotional and dispassionate altogether. Rather than being based on the whim of a capricious and fearsome god, it seems to be expressed by the biblical writers as God's automatic and involuntary response to disobedience.

Some of these writers even speak simply of *the* wrath (meaning God's wrath), without explicitly linking it to him, as if to imply that it is an impersonal force. C.H. Dodd, the British biblical scholar, confused this point, I believe, by suggesting that the wrath is, in fact, an impersonal entity — 'merely an inevitable process of cause and effect in a moral universe'.

I understand his point. He was wanting to emphasise the degree to which God's wrath is not a pouting tantrum, but rather a measured, objective response to moral failure. The fact is, however, as we've noted, that God *does* have a will and his wrath is associated with his ability to 'feel' about the things he observes. (David Pawson, another British minister, once said that if he could hire a sky-writer for a day, the message he would emblazon across the skies would be 'God does have feelings'!)

God's wrath is never entirely dispassionate. I think 'involuntary' or 'automatic' are better terms. Of course, when some biblical writers describe God's wrath, they are inclined to use human/emotional language because we have no other language that could possibly come close to describing God's inability to be unjust.

One such example is Isaiah 30, a compellingly graphic description of godly wrath. The whole chapter is eloquently written. Verses 27 and 28 are a taste:

See, the name of the Lord comes
from afar,
with burning anger and dense
clouds of smoke;
his lips are full of wrath,
and his tongue is a consuming fire.
His breath is like a rushing torrent,
rising up to the neck.
He shakes the nations in the sieve
of destruction;
he places in the jaws of the peoples
a bit that leads them astray.

Sounds pretty emotive, doesn't it? Well, this is a poetic attempt to wrap words around a profound mystery. It is a celebration of a God who is perfectly just and always righteous. This God cannot but be displeased with anything that contravenes his majestic holiness.

In verse 12, we hear why God has responded with such wrath: '. . .because you have rejected this message, relied on oppression, and depended on deceit'. Such human behaviour as oppression or deceit can evoke only one response from God. It is not emotive or belligerent. It is collected and determined. It is God's wrath. And yet, as the writer continues his poem in verse 29, he turns to the human response to the wrath of God:

> And you will sing
> as on the night you celebrate
> a holy festival;
> your hearts will rejoice
> as when people go up with flutes
> to the mountain of the Lord,
> to the Rock of Israel.

If God's wrath was no more than a divine temper tantrum, it would repel and alienate his frightened people. So why does Isaiah, who speaks of God's wrath as being like a 'consuming fire' and a 'rushing torrent', imagine that humans will respond with gladness? Clearly, wrath is not as simple as a violent explosion of God's hostility towards the world. More likely, it is the secure and objective aspects of a just and holy God. And justice and holiness are attractive qualities, not repulsive ones. The poem continues:

> The Lord will cause men to hear
> his majestic voice
> and will make them see his arm
> coming down
> with raging anger and consuming fire,
> with cloudburst, thunderstorm and hail.

In this poem in Isaiah, you can spot all three of the elements of God's holiness that we have already observed: his majesty, his will and his wrath. This line of thinking has been explored by R.C. Zaehner in his provocative book, *Our Savage God*, in which he claims that God must be a terrible God, for otherwise we end up putting evil outside his control. This would be called dualism — the idea that only goodness is in God's domain and evil is in the domain of another. Zaehner argues (rightly so, I think) that God deserves our terror as much as our devotion.

Oscar Wilde wrote in *The Ballad of Reading Gaol*:

Yet each man kills the thing he loves
By each let this be heard. . .
The coward does it with a kiss,
The brave man with a sword.

To which Zaehner responds, 'God certainly kills the things he loves, but the things he loves rejoice to be killed at such a hand.'

☐ *The fourth aspect of God's holiness: righteousness*
The three aspects previously mentioned might be fearfully corrupted and therefore destructive and violent were it not for righteousness. God's majesty, his jealousy and his wrath are all anchored deeply in his righteousness. There have been countless examples of gods and monarchs who have had performed around them great theatrical displays of pomp and ceremony, producing the effect of majesty and stateliness.

Likewise, despots and earthly rulers have exercised free will and absolute control, using their power to subjugate their peoples by displays of wrath. This century alone, we have to look no further than the European dictators of the 'thirties, 'forties and 'fifties, Adolf Hitler, Josef Stalin and Benito Mussolini. All three had dramatic demonstrations of their majesty, jealousy and anger choreographed through the streets and in the stadiums of Berlin, Moscow and Rome — and yet we are now able to say with supreme confidence that none of these men had righteousness as the foundation of their power.

Without righteousness, even God could be nothing more than a capricious, despotic deity, worthy of our fear and our service, but never our love or devotion.

In this regard, I am using the word 'righteousness' as a moral or ethical term. God's will and wrath can be trusted because God will always do what is right. When we ask what is the right or moral thing, we can answer the question not by appealing to some independent ethical standard (as if we might be able to find one), but rather by appealing to the will and nature of God himself. In this way, God's 'rightness', his moral perfection, forms the foundation or the anchor for the other aspects of his holiness.

We can trust the fact that God always wills the right thing, but that's not all there is to the idea of righteousness. In fact, there's quite a bit more to it, which we'll deal with further in the next chapter.

✠ **Summary**

Let's recap. Remember, we are talking about the fact that God is best understood through 'paradoxical truth'. In order to see the paradox of God's nature, we need to embrace the two apparently contradictory truths that God seems both far away and near at hand.

We gave these two truths their traditional names, 'transcendence' and 'immanence'. The Bible has its own terms for these ideas. For transcendence, it uses the word 'holiness' to describe God's greatness. We then noted four ways of viewing his greatness: his majesty, his will, his wrath and his righteousness.

On the one hand, this paradoxical God is like the deepest and darkest part of the deepest, darkest sea. Imagine being dropped into the middle of the Pacific Ocean, with nothing on every horizon but blue sea and thinking of what lies beneath you: nothing but seemingly endless water around you and below you. God is this awesome — and more. He is more, because he has a will and a personality and because he has feelings about our inadequacy and our poor choices and our foolish mistakes.

This God seems too big, too great, too awesome ever to have contact with mere mortals. This God does seem to be watching us from a great distance.

If you ever have the opportunity to enter some of the great cathedrals in Europe, you'll feel remarkably small. These cavernous buildings were designed specifically to dwarf the worshippers, to give them (and now us) a sense of God's majesty. The high ceilings, the enormous pipe organs, the massive stained glass windows, the lofty pulpits and the commanding altars indicate your nothingness by comparison with God's greatness.

At Disneyland, they have an exhibit based on the film, *Honey, I Shrunk The Kids,* where you enter a giant backyard and, for the duration of your stay, feel smaller than an ant among the weeds and the grass and the sprinkler and some kids' toys. It's the same effect. Obviously, Disneyland hasn't created their enormous world to help you sense God's holiness, but the effect of being made to feel tiny and inconsequential is similar to the intentions of the creators of the fantastic religious architecture of Europe.

So far, we have not dealt with the masculinity or femininity of God. We have only begun to look at the traditional theological understandings of God as stored in the biblical stories. By looking at the basic idea of transcendence and then dealing with immanence in the next chapter, we are creating a sketch of the view of God the church is happy to promulgate.

But can you see, ever so slightly, the traces of masculinity in this idea of transcendence? I'm not suggesting that these ideas of dispassionate anger, tough love and dignified aloofness are necessarily masculine traits, but so many men *do* seem to embody these characteristics — or a pale imitation of them. And we will see in the next chapter that the paradoxical idea of God's immanence contains many aspects we usually associate with femininity.

6

THE LOVING, IMMANENT GOD

What divine nearness looks like

> *Personal relationships are a part of the order of the universe. They are a clue to the nature of ultimate reality. The personal is the highest category we know, and it can't be reduced to atoms and molecules. It is a reality in its own right. That's why it's justified to conceive of a personal God, because when we do so we are using the language of the highest kind of reality of which we have any experience.*
>
> Arthur Peacocke
>
> *God is love.*
>
> 1 John 4, verse 16

GOD *CAN* BE KNOWN! HE CAN BE NEAR and intimately involved with his world and its people. And that kind of intimacy with God can make you feel on top of the world! This notion of being close to God is an expression of God's *immanence* and is to be held in tension with everything we've been saying up to this point.

The God who won't be trifled with — the aloof, distant, frightening, majestic, mysterious God in the last chapter — describes a good many of the fathers

125

we grew up with. The other side of the coin will ring many of the bells we normally associated with our mothers.

✠ What true human love is like

Again, like transcendence, immanence is not a biblical term. But the storytellers of the Bible do have their own word. That word is 'love'. It's unfortunate that the word 'love' has been so abused and misused. In fact, I desperately wanted to find another biblical term to describe God's closeness to his people, but clearly this is the best one. We just need to rediscover the original meanings of this simple, often-used term.

To illustrate what I mean by the abuse of the word 'love', let me tell you about a film I saw not that long ago. It's called *Romper Stomper* and it concerns the disintegration of a group of Nazi-inspired skinheads in inner-city Melbourne. These people are almost completely overwhelmed by hatred and violence. They are wantonly destructive; they have no regard for property, life or human dignity. Clearly misoguenous as well as racist, they treat women as property and, even in the act of sexual intercourse, they are violent and brutal.

There is one very explicit sex scene where during the animal-like activity the two characters — who hardly know each other and whose relationship has been based on brutality and hatred — pant and heave the words 'I love you, I love you' over and over. It is as if the act of sexual gratification necessarily implies that love is involved.

Many people have been deeply offended by the

racism and the graphic violence depicted in this film. I was more stung by the fact that 'love' has become another word for frenzied, selfish and aggressive displays of sexual satisfaction. Clearly, the characters in this film (without exception) had no notion whatsoever about the real meaning of love.

But even those of us who have never shaved our heads for the neo-Nazi cause still find ourselves using the term 'love' in all sorts of inappropriate ways. We 'love' ice-cream. We'd 'love' to go to the beach today, thanks. We 'love' the music of Van Morrison. And we are even capable of making the same mistake as the characters in *Romper Stomper* by assuming that a strong sexual/emotional feeling for a member of the opposite sex necessitates the use of the phrase 'I love you'.

Scott Peck's work on defining love has been extremely helpful. He makes this suggestion:

> *Of all the misconceptions about love, the most powerful and pervasive is the belief that 'falling in love' is love or at the very least one of the manifestations of love. It is a potent misconception, because falling in love is subjectively experienced in a very powerful fashion as an experience of love.*[1]

Now, there's nothing wrong with the fabulous hormonal rush that comes with the infatuation of 'falling in love', but this does not necessarily equate with love itself. He goes on to explain further:

> *The experience of falling in love is specifically a sex-linked erotic experience. We do not fall in love with our children*

even though we may love them very deeply. . . We fall in love only when we are consciously or unconsciously sexually motivated.[2]

Peck also suggests that falling in love never lasts for any great length of time. The feeling of ecstatic lovingness that accompanies the experience of falling in love always passes. In fact, he believes that real loving begins after the *feelings* of love have passed, though he admits that without the feelings to begin with we'd probably not have the energy for the engagement or connection in the first place.

However, I think it should be noted that, while a film like *Romper Stomper* is deplored by many for its violence, it makes no pretence at really depicting genuine loving. The scene to which I referred earlier is startling because any discerning viewer will be repulsed by an act that he/she knows is not really love at all.

More offensive to me is a film like the very popular *Pretty Woman* which many people find charming and romantic as if it does depict genuine loving. In fact, it's the story of a man who buys a very beautiful woman for a week and in the course of the ensuing days plays out his psycho-erotic feelings towards her. He tells her what to wear, how to behave, how to eat in public. Under these very demeaning circumstances, they somehow manage to 'fall in love'.

It's not genuine loving at all. It would be okay, I guess, if the film had no illusions about this, but it now occupies a place as one of the great cinematic love stories. Believe me, *Pretty Woman* is no more about love than

Romper Stomper. It's about dependence, control and manipulation.

So not only is the wild, romantic, exciting phenomenon of falling in love not real love, but it is impossible to love anything other than another person. There is actually a process of attraction and incorporation that can embrace objects and activities which might be called love, but genuine love always involves the extension and spiritual growth of the beloved.

To love someone is to seek their wholeness, to desire their growth. It is to seek the best for another person, to seek to allow the other person to blossom and become the best person they could possibly, in their uniqueness, become. By 'loving', I am referring to the commitment to act creatively into the life of another so that they can grow spiritually — including emotionally, intellectually, socially — to become their true self as created by God.

In other words, you can't love chocolate, football, your car or your favourite television program. You *can* love anyone to whom you make the kind of commitment outlined above which may or may not come with pleasant feelings at times. It's obvious, then, that Richard Gere doesn't love Julia Roberts — in fact, much of the 'love' depicted on screen falls short on the basis of this definition. Our definition does mean, however, that we can behave in a loving fashion toward close friends and new acquaintances, to work colleagues and sporting competitors, to our children and to the children of others, to our partners and to those whose company we dislike.

Jesus, by calling us to love others, doesn't anticipate that we will conjure up warm feelings about everyone (including our enemies, as Jesus also pointed out), but that we will *determine* to behave lovingly nonetheless. Love, therefore, is a doing word. It is more like a verb than a noun.

✠ What God's love is like

Now, up to this point we have been talking about human love in an attempt to reclaim the lost concept of genuine loving. Using this as a springboard, let's take a look at God's divine loving and see the way it counters and holds in tension all that we mentioned in the previous chapter about God's holiness. I think you'll see that God's love is robust and relentless. It is not about control or manipulation. It is not impatient or self-seeking. It is God's commitment to act creatively in our lives for our own growth and potential wholeness.

Both the Old Testament and the New use the term 'love' to describe God's intimate dealings with humankind. In the language of the Old Testament, which is Hebrew, and the language of the New Testament, which is Greek, there are several words that we translate into English as 'love'. They each indicate different aspects or types of love but, in each case, when applied to God, tell us something about the way he relates to us. Unfortunately, we English readers are hamstrung by having only one term which is supposed to contain all the richness and depth of meaning associated with the idea of love.

Just as I admitted that it is impossible to describe the transcendence of God, so I'll admit my inability to do justice to God's love. His closeness and intimacy with people is too difficult to communicate unless it's been experienced. But let me begin by offering one man's experience of God's intimate loving. His name is Martin Luther King:

> *The agonising moments through which I have passed during the last few years have also drawn me closer to God. More than ever before, I am convinced of the reality of a personal God. True, I have always believed in the personality of God. But in the past, the idea of a personal God was nothing more than a. . . theologically and philosophically satisfying [idea]. Now it is a living reality that has been validated in the experiences of everyday life. God has been profoundly real to me in recent years. In the midst of lonely days and dreary nights I have heard an inner voice saying, 'Lo, I will be with you.'* [3]

This nearness of God is as much a reality as the transcendence of God. Both realities are equally true. Dr King has described an experience that millions throughout the ages have shared. It is an experience that brings comfort, relief, warmth and security. These feelings are in direct contrast to the human response to God's majesty, for example, which evokes insecurity, fear and uncertainty. Here we are beginning to catch the power of paradox in understanding God. His majesty repels us to some degree, while his love has the reverse effect: it draws us nearer to him.

But if the immanence of God is merely some romantic emotional feeling, then hasn't it become no more

than the feelings of falling in love that come so far short
of genuine loving? How might we better describe God's
loving immanence? For the sake of balance, let's look
at four aspects of God's love to hold in tension with the
four aspects of his holiness.

☐ *First, God's love involves righteousness*

To really understand God's immanence/love, we need
to go back to the concept we began to examine in the
previous chapter: righteousness. While righteousness
was the fourth aspect of God's holiness, it ought to be
the first aspect of his love.

You see, righteousness underpins the other aspects of
God's holiness, but it overarches all the ways of describing God's love. Remember that I defined righteousness
as God's *rightness* on moral/ethical grounds. Well, it
means even more than that. It also refers very specifically to God's way of relating to humankind.

In the Old Testament, God's righteousness is based
on his commitment to his people and in his saving acts
towards them. Against all the odds, God remains in a
loving relationship with humankind. He is faithful in
all relationships and keeps all his promises. In Isaiah 41,
verse 10, God expresses it in this way:

> *So do not fear, for I am with you;*
> *do not be dismayed, for I am your God.*
> *I will strengthen you and help you;*
> *I will uphold you with my righteous hand.*

Here we see God's immanence clearly expressed by

the idea of righteousness. In other words, the righteousness of God is the very quality that draws him near to his people in their hour of need. But not only is righteousness expressive of God's commitment to humankind. It is also the motivation for his acts of salvation. Isaiah continues:

Your heavens above rain down
 righteousness;
let the clouds shower it down.
Let the earth open wide,
let salvation spring up,
let righteousness grow with it;
I, the Lord, have created it.

So his people can trust that his word is his bond and can base their own lives on his faithfulness. Therefore, righteousness refers, first, to doing the right thing (holiness) and, second, to doing things right (love).

☐ *Second, God's love involves loyalty*
The Hebrew word for this loyal kind of love is *'chesed'* (the 'ch' sound should be pronounced as if you're clearing your throat). I should point out that *chesed* is not necessarily directly translated as 'loyal love'. It conveys the sense of unfailing, steadfast love, an unshakeable regard for the loved on the part of the lover. But I think 'loyalty' is as good a word as any. When used in the Old Testament (234 times, mind you), it indicates God's consistent, reliable allegiance and willingness to do good on behalf of humankind.

God remains loyal to his people because he can't do

anything else. It is God's involuntary, almost automatic response to human beings. He *must* remain loyal in his love for us. This loyalty is not shown merely out of appreciation for human worship (as if God needed his ego salved every Sunday with our 'flattery') or out of any divine self-interest. There is nothing in it for him. His loyal love is demonstrated on the basis of his firm determination to do so.

It's not until the New Testament that we find the dramatic theological statement, 'God is love' (1 John 4, verse 16), which is based on the Old Testament belief that God is by his very nature unable to be unloving.

This reminds me of the story American writer, Calvin Miller, tells of the little girl who is watching her father cut down a tree in their backyard. As her dad lays the axe into the trunk of the tree, the girl spies wood chips flying in every direction. Lifting one from the grass, she calls out to her father with incredulity, 'Look, Dad, trees have wood in 'em!'

Well, we know that trees don't have wood *in* them. Trees *are* wood. Likewise with God. He doesn't have love *in* him. He *is* love. He doesn't choose to love. It is the very 'stuff' of God that means he can't help but be loving.

Now, recall that when we talk about love, we are not meaning that warm, fuzzy, goose-pimply feeling of 'falling in love' experienced by Richard Gere and Julia Roberts in *Pretty Woman*. When we use this word in relation to God, we are meaning something much tougher and more dependable. Do you recall in the previous chapter talking about God's will as being expressed through his tough kind of jealousy, the refusal to be trifled with or ignored or rejected by humankind? In the face of such rejection, we discover a God who refuses to abandon his people.

It reminds me of the person who, for the past forty-five years, has marked the birthday of Edgar Allen Poe by leaving cognac and roses on his grave. Every year on 19 January, in the dead of a winter's night, a mystery man in a dark coat and a trilby has entered a Baltimore graveyard and placed half a bottle of cognac and three red roses on the writer's grave. The roses are believed to represent the poet, his wife Virginia and his mother Maria Clemm, all of whom are buried in the small cemetery. Poe died aged forty in 1849. His dying words reputedly were: 'Lord, help my poor soul.'

And every year, the curator of the Edgar Allen Poe Museum in Baltimore watches from the church, never attempting to stop or identify the mystery mourner as he keeps his appointment, rain, hail or shine. That kind of resolve and devotion is so touching and so rare. Perhaps that's why, every year in newspapers all over the world, it's reported that the mystery man has kept his appointment once more. Loyalty and faithfulness are rare commodities. Even if it's a single column on page twelve, people still look on 20 January to see if the mystery man had returned the previous day with his touching gift of cognac and roses.

This is the same kind of robust resolve that God exhibits in his dealings with his people. Like the man in the trilby, he fulfils his promises and keeps his appointments forever. Here is a God who is not motivated by the insecure need to be adored, but by the unshakeable loyalty of *chesed*-love. In other words, just as God's majestic transcendence is held in tension with his loving immanence, so is his jealousy to be held in tension with his loyalty. There will be times when our conduct evokes in God a response of uncompromising jealousy, but this is always held in check (so to speak) by his relentless loyalty toward us.

Here in Sydney we have a football team called the North Sydney Bears. They have been Sydney's perpetual losers, last winning the competition way back in the 'twenties. Their trophy cabinet must be the barest in Sydney. Graced with a delightful old pitch surrounded by majestic palm trees and a stadium protected by the National Trust, the Bears only ever drew a crowd when nearby Manly, one of the super teams of the competition, plays them at North Sydney Oval.

Then a miracle occurred. In the 'nineties, something inexplicable began to happen. The Bears started winning! Up to the point of my writing this, they still haven't actually won the premiership, but they've started to go very close. And along with all this came another miracle: Bears supporters started coming out of the woodwork. It became extremely fashionable to be able to say that you'd barracked for Norths all these lean years. Television personalities and politicians suddenly began to wear the red and black strip and sing the praises of 'their' team.

You see, everyone loves the underdog as long as he has a slim chance of winning. When the Bears had no chance of winning anything other than the wooden spoon, let alone becoming finalists, no-one wanted to know them. As soon as they looked like pulling off an upset, all these fair-weather supporters came forth.

There were some, of course, who did stick by the Bears through those seventy lean years. They were the loyal ones, the 'true believers', the real diehards. These, the staunchest of fans, deserve a medal for hanging in there. God's loyalty is not dissimilar. He'll back you every step of the way, even during the lean years. But there's absolutely nothing in it for him. His loyalty benefits one party only: the loved rather than the lover.

In the Old Testament, this is expressed in his devotion to Israel. Of course, there had been times in Israel's history when she was the winning team, feted by nations from around the ancient Near East. During those halceon days, everyone wanted to be known as a supporter of the great nation of Israel. But it was during the many, many lean years that God proved his staunch diehard *chesed*-love.

When Israel had been defeated and lay in ruins, its people in exile in a foreign land, the prophet Isaiah gave voice to God's loyal love by dreaming of the day when God would restore the nation. Isaiah 54, verse 10 is a dramatic testimonial of divine steadfast love:

Though the mountains be shaken
 and the hills be removed,
yet my unfailing love for you will
 not be shaken
nor my covenant of peace be removed,
says the Lord who has
 compassion on you.

God is like the father who demands unswerving allegiance, who is 'jealous' in his desire for complete devotion, but he is also like the mother who remains loyal and steadfast to her children no matter how much they may disappoint her.

How many times in film and television and in our own experience have we seen the image of the father who says, 'That's it! I've taken about as much as I can possibly take. That kid has got to go. I won't have such behaviour going on under my roof!', only to hear the mother plead the case of her wayward child. Her devotion and loyalty towards her child knows no bounds. Well, God is *both* parents equally and at the same time.

❒ *Third, God's love involves mercy*
Mercy is held in tension with God's wrath. Are you getting the picture? Each aspect of God's holiness is in tension with each aspect of his love: his majesty is held in tension with his intimacy with his people; his jealousy is held in tension with his loyalty; and his wrath is to be equally synthesised with his mercy.

I mentioned earlier that God's wrath is his right and proper response to human disobedience. God is involuntarily drawn to condemn human inadequacy. A morally perfect, unblemished, majestic God cannot come into contact with imperfection without being drawn to destroy (or put right) that which is wrong. This makes it difficult for him to be intimate or loyally predisposed to humankind when we are clearly imperfect. That's where this third aspect of godly love comes in. His divine anger or wrath can only be truly understood when seen in the light of his mercy. Since God is love, he cannot but be both loyal and merciful.

The old Hebrew word for 'mercy' comes from their term for bowels, since it was believed that there rested the seat of compassion in much the same way as today we talk about love coming from someone's heart. We know that love is not produced by the organ that beats away inside our chests, but we still talk about 'giving our heart away' to someone we adore. The Hebrews believed that since compassion, mercy and forgiveness were such profound emotions, they must emit from the deepest recesses of our bodies.

When used in the Old Testament, mercy referred to the deep, tender feeling of compassion that is evoked by the helplessness, the vulnerability, the suffering or the weakness of another in need. Unlike the word for loyal love, *chesed*, which is almost exclusively used in reference to God, *raham* (mercy) could refer to the compassion a parent feels for his/her child, a mother feels for her baby or a lover for the beloved. But when referring to God, it indicated his desire to preserve and help those in distress, to redeem those who are lost and to forgive, heal and give life. And surely, the roles of healer and comforter and life-giver are roles we have normally assigned more to our mothers than our fathers.

When linked to his loyal love, mercy could never fail. It was always available. Even God's righteous anger at the blatant disobedience of humankind could not cancel out his commitment to be loyal and merciful towards us. Speaking of a time when Israel abandoned their faith in

God, in Nehemiah 9, verse 17, Nehemiah says:

> *They refused to listen and failed to remember the miracles you performed among them. They became stiff-necked and, in their rebellion, appointed a leader in order to return to their slavery. But you are a forgiving God, gracious and compassionate, slow to anger and abounding in love. Therefore you did not desert them. . .*

Notice that in the case Nehemiah outlines above, there is no plea on the part of God's people for clemency. They are a 'stiff-necked' people — an old-fashioned term meaning to be arrogant and unyeilding — and have disregarded God's rightful place as a jealous ruler. The fact that God offers mercy without even being asked indicates the potency of his love.

That love is unconditional. In a world where every god had its price, the God of Israel will love and love and love. He is a forgiving God, 'gracious and compassionate, slow to anger and abounding in love'. Does this sound like a different God to the one who is jealous and uncompromising, majestic and holy, frightening and wrathful? Remember Isaiah's description of God's anger as rolling thunder and his wrath like scorching winds? Had Nehemiah and Isaiah gone to different Sunday schools? Did they get their stories wrong? Far from it!

You see, Isaiah was just as capable of sketching the loving and compassionate nature of God as was Nehemiah of his fearful and awe-inspiring holiness. They had grasped the complexity of the paradoxical nature of God. A god who is all loving never demands our respect or our service. A god who is all holiness never evokes our devotion or our worship. When both can be true, held in tension, we can come closer to the fully realised image of the God that the Bible and traditional theology offer us.

☐ Fourth, God's love involves God's favour

This is the aspect that holds God's *rightness* in tension. God's holiness means he is always right, remember? We can be assured that his majesty, his jealousy and his wrath will always be expressed or enacted in a morally and ethically perfect way.

If this was truly the case, God might well have wiped humankind off the face of the earth. We are not 'right'. We are flawed, tainted, mistake-prone. In many cases, we are violent, arrogant, bigoted and depraved. If God always acted in the right way, we would not survive his wrath. It is his favour towards humankind that stays his hand of fury. He still responds to disobedience with wrath. But it is a wrath that is always held in tension with his loving favour.

In the Bible, the term 'favour' is strongly connected with the human face — just as 'mercy' is with the bowels. To be shown somebody's face or to be granted an audience, especially with an important leader, was to receive their favour. As a result, many of the phrases in the Old Testament that speak of God's favour have the word 'face' as a component.

In many churches these days, a commonly recited benediction (the closing words of a service of worship) implores God to 'make his face to shine upon you, to lift up the light of his countenance upon you'. I guess many people have sat in church and had that invocation said over them without really understanding its significance. Basically, it means to invite God to show his favour to you.

So 'to lift up the face' is usually translated in the Bible as 'to win the favour of'. And another interesting expression, 'to make the face of one pleasant', means to try to turn someone's hostility into hospitality. It virtually means to win someone over. The same is true in prayer when the faithful seek to gain the face or favour of God. The assumption is that when God hears his people, he turns his face towards them. This might seem very simplistic to apparently sophisticated thinkers today. We know God doesn't literally have a face with two eyes, a nose and a mouth, but I think there's some real value in using anthropomorphic language in order to comprehend the nature of God.

Something I used to do too often was to look away when someone was talking to me. I wasn't meaning to be rude. I think it's because I'm a more auditory person than a visual person. I could quite happily carry on a decent conversation while staring at the carpet or into space. It really didn't bother me but, as you can imagine, it drove other people to distraction, especially my wife, Carolyn.

She is a marriage and family counsellor, so her listening skills are very highly developed. For her, the way you sit when listening, the expression on your face, where you place your hands all have considerable bearing on the therapeutic value of the conversation. For this reason, she couldn't stand it when I seemed so oblivious to these skills. I had assumed for years that listening was something you do exclusively with your ears. Not so. Carolyn has helped me see that you can, in fact, listen more effectively with your whole body — and in particular with your face.

Looking into the speaker's face, connecting with his or her eyes, nodding with affirmation at appropriate times, offering empathic facial expressions are as crucial to the process of listening as having your ears cleaned out. Even children know this is true. Have you ever noticed that when a young child has something really important to say, they will grasp your face in their hands and force you to look at them? To lift up your face to one who is in need indicates your favour, your interest, your concern. And hurting individuals find it almost irresistible to respond to someone who shows this kind of love.

This seems to be exactly what the Hebrews had in mind when they sang praises about their God's *favouritism*. In the Psalms — and Psalm 5, verse 12 is a good example — we hear that God's favour protects his people like a shield, helping them to endure difficult circumstances beyond their normal capacity to do so. It was also their great dream that one day in the future God would restore their national pride, reconstitute their flagging religious zeal and offer salvation to all the nations. This was appropriately called 'a time of favour'.

Isaiah 49, verses 8 and 9a describes it this way:

This is what the Lord says:
'In the time of my favour I will   answer you,

and in the day of salvation I will help you;
I will keep you and will make you
to be a covenant for the people,
to restore the land
and to reassign its desolate inheritances,
to say to the captives, Come out,
and to those in darkness, Be free.

Now, when we consider that God's holiness is underpinned by righteousness — that he will always do the right and just thing when exercising his wrath — we can see how contrary this is to this kind of favouritism. God's 'rightness' is held in tension with his loving favour. In this regard, God is never completely fair. If he was fair, his people would have suffered far greater deprivation and punishment for their failures than has been the case.

Like a mother whose unquenchable love for her babies causes her to forgive them beyond the call of duty even when they wrong her, so is God. He is so loving that he desires above all to show his favour, to lift up his face to those he calls his children. This is yet further evidence of the paradoxical nature of God as understood in traditional theology.

The transcendent aspect to God's nature echoes many of the traits we often equate with masculinity or fatherhood. And the immanent aspect can't help but remind us of the loyal, dogged, unrelenting love of the mother who always shows patience, forgiveness, tenderness, mercy and comfort.

So you see, even in traditional, biblical theology these two sides to God seap through. God is both father and mother, both holy and loving. And each side holds the other in tension. Each side of God's paradoxical nature makes the other possible.

This means that the biblical expressions of this paradox always maintain the synthesis. Therefore, God's majesty holds his intimacy in tension. God's jealousy is held in tension with his loyalty. And his wrath is to be synthesised with his mercy. And finally, his rightness is held in tension with his favouritism.

✠ Ancient stories that hold the paradoxes of God in tension

Now, this might all sound okay in theory, but what does it look like when human beings encounter a God who is both masculine and feminine, both holy and loving, both transcendent and immanent at the same time? What does the tension about which we've been speaking look like in the course of human affairs? For this, I can direct you to two fabulous stories in the Old Testament. They each concern God encountering men with the unique combination of overwhelming holiness and genuine loving.

Before I retell them, I need to point out two important details. First, not every story in the Bible about human-divine relationships so neatly juxtaposes the transcendence and immanence of God as do these stories. Many of the historical anecdotes deal exclusively with God's nearness, his intimate devotion to his people, and many others deal exclusively with his awesome majesty. But occasionally we come across a passage that so deftly marries both these elements that it's almost too good to be true.

One section of the Bible that manages such a marriage is the series of stories called the Exodus, which relate both God's majestic power in releasing the Jews from the bondage of Egypt (you might have seen the Charlton Heston version on TV!) and his loyal love in staying near to them in the wilderness. In fact, these stories are among the most celebrated in the Jewish faith-community. I think that's because the stories so clearly maintain the tension between God's immanence and transcendence.

The second point we must make is that, while these two stories deal with *men* encountering God, I don't want to appear to be implying that an encounter with the divine is a right reserved exclusively for the male of our species. There are plenty of stories in the Bible about women meeting with God (admittedly, there are more about men, but this says something more about ancient Hebrew society than about God's predeliction for male company). But the stories I am about to retell illustrate all that I've said up to this point so perfectly that I couldn't possibly not use them; they just happen to concern men. That's not an apology — just a note of clarification.

So prepare yourself to see just a glimpse of the masculine/feminine, transcendent/immanent, holy/loving God in intercourse with humankind.

◻ *First, the story of Elijah's encounter with God*
  on Mt Carmel and Mt Horeb
The first of our two stories concerns that fiery old Jewish prophet, Elijah. He was a belligerent old goat,

who for most of his life refused to take a backward step in his defense of the God of Israel.

Towards the end of his career as God's mouthpiece to the Jewish nation, he performed one of the riskiest and, in many ways, the most comical demonstrations of God's power when he challenged the prophets of another god, Ba'al, to a religious duel.

Related for us in 1 Kings 18, the story recounts how Elijah became fed up with the people wavering between whichever god seemed to suit their purposes best on any given day, and he demanded they choose once and for all. He gathered all the cultic priests and prophets on Mount Carmel and set up two altars, one for Ba'al and one for the God of Israel. On each altar, he placed a bull as a sacrifice to each respective deity. Then, with the whole nation watching, he challenged the other prophets to implore their god to send down fire from the heavens to consume their offering and to confirm that Ba'al is the only true god. Some contest!

All day the cultic priests prayed and sang, ranted and raved, conducting bizarre rituals in order to incite their god to display his power. All along, fiesty old Elijah said things like, 'Shout louder. Surely he is a god! Perhaps he's deep in thought or busy or on holiday. Maybe he's having a nap and needs to be woken!'

In the end, nothing comes of all their carrying on. Then Elijah, not content simply to show them up, has his God's altar and his offering thoroughly doused with water. He even digs a trench around the altar to catch the run-off. Then, before the prophets and priests, the people and their rulers, he calls down fire from heaven as a confirmation of the authenticity and authority of his God.

As the stone altar is scorched and the drenched wood and the dead beast consumed by a fierce fire storm, the people finally fall down and confess God as their only master. After which Elijah, not a faint-hearted man by any stretch of the imagination, has the hundreds of prophets slaughtered in the valley below. Phew!

But this isn't the part of the story that excites me. What happens later is even more interesting. After his flashy display, Elijah discovered that the queen, Jezebel, who had been a loyal patron of the prophets of Ba'al, planned to do him in for having humiliated and destroyed them. So he bolts. He runs in terror from the wrath of Jezebel. She must have been some lady! Elijah can stand in front of the whole nation and make a laughing stock of 850 priests and dare to call down fire from the sky but, when he hears Jezebel is cross with him, he takes off.

He fled to Beersheba in Judah, then travelled a day's journey into the wilderness, after which he travelled a further forty days to the distant Mount Horeb. He slept that night in a cave. And it's what happened to him there on that mountain that is so impressive. It is in I Kings 19, verses 9 to 11. Listen:

> And the word of the Lord came to him: 'What are you doing here, Elijah?'
> He replied, 'I have been very zealous for the Lord God Almighty. The Israelites have rejected your covenant, broken down your altars, and put your prophets to death with the sword. I am the only one left and now they are trying

> *to kill me, too.*
> *The Lord said, 'Go out and stand on the mountain in the*
> *presence of the Lord, for the Lord is about to pass by.'*

Can you believe this? After all his flashy, macho bravado, after all his preaching and persuasion, nothing has changed in Israel. The people still have no regard for God. God says that Elijah — broken, humbled, disillusioned and confused — will be allowed to see him face to face. Here is the amazing story of a man who is about to gaze at the face of God. I think you'll be surprised by what he sees (verses 11 and 12):

> *Then a great and powerful wind tore the mountain apart*
> *and shattered the rocks before the Lord. . . but the Lord*
> *was not in the wind.*
> *After the wind there was an earthquake. . . but the Lord*
> *was not in the earthquake.*
> *After the earthquake came a fire. . . but the Lord was not*
> *in the fire.*

What greater displays of God's awesome majesty and power could you expect? Earth, wind and fire! Hurricanes, earthquakes and fires are surely more than adequate expressions of God's transcendence and holiness. Here is the frightening, savage God, the tough-posturing, masculine God, flexing his muscles with divine macho power expressed through the most devastating of earthly powers — earth, wind and fire.

And yet God is not fully revealed in these things. Even though these most dreadful of natural disasters have wrent Mount Horeb apart and no doubt put Elijah out of his mind with fear, God has still not appeared completely. But when he does, it is in the most unlikely way, as verse 12 records: 'And after the fire came a gentle whisper.' In some older translations it reads, 'a still, small voice'. In the midst of such calamity and chaos, God is revealed as a gentle whisper, like the cooing of a lover in one's ear.

Elijah, who has huddled in terror in the debris of what's left of his cave, covers his face with his cloak and ventures forth. There he has the very same conversation with God that took place earlier. God asks what he's doing in the wilderness, to which Elijah spells out the desperate situation in Israel. Then God commands him to return to Israel and anoint a new king, Jehu, and a successor to his own role as prophet, Elisha. Filled with new courage, the old man returns to fulfil his final duties as God's servant.

Why is this story so significant? Because when God chooses to reveal himself in all his fullness, we see both aspects of his nature: his terrifying holiness and his gentle, still, whispered expressions of love. And the only appropriate human response to this kind of seduction — for surely that's what it is — is to be filled with courage and new resolve while still quaking inwardly.

❒ *Second, the story of Job's encounter with God*
The second story is even better known than this. It concerns a man named Job, who lived at a time in Israel's history when the Jews were being tricked into thinking the same way as the pagan nations.

The pagans believed in a pantheon of gods who resided in the heavens and who sent down either blessings (good fortune) or curses (bad fortune), depending upon the faithfulness of the people or the mood of the gods.

In this kind of equation, it's easy to tell who is faithful and who is not: those to whom good things happen must be okay and those to whom bad things happen must *not* be okay. It's very simple, isn't it? Except that it's poor logic, because it meant that the rich and the well-born, the powerful and the strong were always assumed to be the spiritually elite. It's simply nothing less than bigotry to judge a person's spirituality on the basis of their personal circumstances. Well, Israel was beginning to think the same of their God.

The radical nature of Job's story is that it sets up a situation in which a good, upright, wealthy, well-born individual has the most astounding calamities befall him. In other words, he doesn't fit the equation. Most of the book concerns Job and his friends trying to make sense of why bad things were happening to a good man. His friends' only option seemed to be to conclude that Job couldn't have been as good and faithful a man as they all had once believed. Job's trauma arises out of his conviction that he really is a faithful man experiencing agonising misfortune.

After an extensive debate between the characters in the story, suddenly God appears to set things in perspective. One of the major themes in the book of Job is a call to return to the Hebrew belief that God is revealed through suffering rather than being absent in it (which the pagans believed). God's dramatic entrance at the end of the book affirms the ideal that misfortune and calamity ought to draw the sufferer nearer to God rather than indicating that God has withdrawn.

In chapter 38, verses 1 to 3, God enters the stage:

> *Then the Lord answered Job out of the storm. He said:*
> *'Who is this that darkens my counsel with words without*
> *knowledge? Brace yourself like a man: I will question you*
> *and you will answer me!'*

His stern introduction is fitting, for Job and his friends have been daring to question God for over thirty chapters. It's time God had his say. But he chooses to reveal himself not through formulas or propositions, but through questions. There are over seventy questions asked by God of Job that follow, all of which Job has no way of answering. The following, in chapter 38, verses 2 to 7, are a sample:

> *'Where were you when I laid*
> *the earth's foundation?*
> *Tell me, if you understand.*
> *Who marked off its dimensions?*
> *Surely you know!*
> *Who stretched out a measuring line*
> *across it?*
> *On what were its footings set,*
> *or who laid its cornerstone ----*
> *while the morning stars sang together*
> *and all the angels shouted for joy?'*

It goes on and on in this line of questioning. God asks about the dimensions of the earth, the formation of the stars, the mating habits of sea creatures and mountain-dwelling animals, the nesting habits of the greater birds. These might be things we could answer with the use of the *Encyclopaedia Brittanica*, but in Job's day these were among the greatest mysteries of the world.

In other words, God's holiness is dramatically splashed across the canvas in the form of one natural mystery after another. God even asks about the great constellations of the northern sky, indicating that even the wondrous and unfathomable heavens crowded with innumerable stars is a mere trifling to him. He knows every star and has counted every stellar light. Even on earth, the mysterious habits of the wild horse, the ostrich and the mountain goat are seen by God, though known to no man at that time.

Job responds in chapter 40, verses 1 and 5, in fear:

I am unworthy ---- how can I reply
  to you?
I put my hand over my mouth.
I spoke once, but I have no answer ----
  twice, but I will say no more.

But this is not God's desired response. His very masculine posturing, his strong interest in demonstrating his greater knowledge (also a very masculine trait) might elicit fear, it might intimidate, but this is not all God wants from Job. Whilst it might be natural to be afraid in the presence of the holy, fear alone is not the most appropriate way to encounter the divine. This God is not content with mute fear. So he goes on, etching the finer details across the canvas, filling in the broader brushstrokes until the picture becomes clearer.

He continues with yet further questions this time about the leviathan and the behemoth, frightening mythical creatures (believed to be based on the elephant and the crocodile) whose fearful exploits were recounted in the local lore of Job's world. What God is this, who is not only familiar with the most secret details of the animal kingdom, the solar system, the tides and the planetary movements, but who can also recount the intimate and unknowable features of the most terrifying sea and land monsters?

The dawning of the ultimate truth — that God, though so holy and fearful, still takes the time to reveal himself to Job, a mere mortal — finally occurs to our hero. Job realises that this is love: the God who knows every detail of the universe also knows and cares for me! He is awestruck. His simple retort in chapter 42, verses 2 and 5, is a delightful proclamation of worship:

> *I know that you can do all things;*
> *no plan of yours can be thwarted.*
> *You asked, 'Who is this that*
> *obscures my counsel without knowledge?'*
> *Surely I spoke of things I did not understand,*
> *things too wonderful for me to know.*
> *You said, 'Listen now, and I will speak;*
> *I will question you,*
> *and you shall answer me.'*
> *My ears had heard of you,*
> *but now my eyes have seen you.*

For God, it's one thing for you to have *heard of* him, or *about* him. But it's an entirely different thing to have *seen* him in his fullness as Job had now done. Too many of us have heard half of what there is to know about him, but it's time we opened our eyes to all of him.

The great psychologist/mystic, Carl Jung, once wrote a fascinating book called *Answers To Job*, in which he claimed that we must resist the temptation to discard the dark side to God. The relationship between God's love and his rage, between his loyalty and his jealousy, between his femininity and his masculinity, shouldn't be regarded as an irreconcilable split in God's schizophrenic nature, but as indispensable opposites.

Says Jung: 'God is not only to be loved, but also to be feared. He fills us with evil as well as good.' By evil, I take him to mean such things as horror, brokenness, punishment and disillusionment. In being touched by God, we must be prepared for a Being who is both light and darkness, both frightening and comforting, both masculine and feminine. To do otherwise is to ignore both the complexity of our own natures and the mystery of God.

So we can see, even in traditional, biblical theology, that the masculine and feminine sides of God have always been there. The same 'macho God' who can strut and display himself as the mover of earth, wind and fire can also whisper tenderly in our ears.

We lose far too much and gain very little when we abandon balance in our understanding of this paradoxical God. If only we could rediscover and unleash the feminine face of God, we would be serious about allowing God to whisper seductively in our ear, to truly touch us all.

7

GOD AND FEMININITY

How divine 'completeness' includes the feminine

> *For, ah, who can express*
> *How full of bonds and simpleness*
> *Is God,*
> *How narrow is He,*
> *And how the wide, waste field of possibility*
> *Is only trod*
> *Straight to His homestead in the human heart,*
> *And all His art*
> *Is as the babe's that wins his Mother to repeat*
> *Her little song so sweet!*
>
> Coventry Patmore

> *When God made man, she was having one of her off days.*
> Anonymous

I'VE MENTIONED SEVERAL TIMES THAT THE TWO SIDES to God's nature — transcendence and immanence — echo the different ways men and women respond to their worlds. I have avoided suggesting that transcendence is a divine masculine trait or immanence a divine feminine trait, because technically I don't think they are. However, I am prepared to allow that these two sides of this paradoxical God do hint at God's masculinity and his femininity.

In chapter 2, we observed these basic movements of human sexuality — that for men meaningful existence is expressed in terms of separation, individualism and achievement, and for women intimacy, bonding and interrelationships are more meaningful. In fact, we characterised these as 'entering' and 'inviting', or as 'achieving' and 'attaching'.

Well, surely on the basis of the stories we've looked at in traditional theology, it's not difficult to see that God is capable of these movements. When we speak of God as transcendent, we are referring to the holy, separate God. He is complete. He has mastery over his world and rules with confidence and independence. In this regard, God reflects the so-called masculine movement. He is the epitome of everything a man desires to be. I happen to think there are others ways he is masculine, also, and we'll explore these later.

✠ The feminine face of God

On the other hand, it's not a great leap to see that we have spoken of God in very feminine terms, also. The loving, intimate God detailed in the previous chapter is concerned with attachment and involvement, about relationships and independence. Whereas the holy God can get along very well without us, thankyou very much, the loving God couldn't bear to think of a world without us. In this regard, God is particularly feminine.

This feminine side can be illustrated by something

I saw on the TV program *Wide World of Sports* when the Ironman contest is telecast from Hawaii. This is a quite remarkable event. Each contestant must complete three legs of what is surely the most gruelling race on earth. The first section is a 3.8 kilometre swim. That's about seventy-five laps of an Olympic-size pool — you could count me out in the first leg! Then, the participants must ride a bicycle for a mere 180 kilometres. That's roughly the distance from Sydney to Newcastle, a trip I regularly make and still complain about when it takes around two hours — in a car. And finally, they must run for forty-two kilometres to the finish line.

Now, it's not as though they have all the time in the world to complete these legs. There are time limits on all three sections, so if you don't make each one, you're out of the race.

Watching this on TV, I saw someone who so perfectly fulfils what we've been discussing that I must tell you about him. He is in his late forties/early fifties, with a son in his late teens/early twenties. His son is severely physically disabled with cerebral palsy and is unable to walk. What this man did was to complete the Ironman competition in Hawaii by *carrying* his son all the way around the course.

For the swim leg, he put his boy in a rubber dinghy of sorts and, harnessing himself to the dinghy, dragged him the whole 3.8 kilometeres. For the bike ride, he had a bicycle custom-built with a large seat in front for his son. And for the run, he pushed his boy in what looked like a big pram all the way to the finish line.

The remarkable thing is that he just made each leg

under the allotted time. And this got many of the officials thinking. If he could complete the course under time with his adult son in tow, what could he do on his own? When asked this, the man responded by saying, 'Alone? What would be the point?' For him, completing the course wasn't any great achievement, but completing it with his *son* was worth all the agony. It's a deeply moving true story of a man who models what God is like.

God can complete the race quite easily without us. He can exhibit mastery and control. He's a winner. But for him there would be no point in doing it alone. He wants to complete it with us in tow. He desires achievement and attachment. As St Augustine once said, 'Without Him, we cannot; without us, He will not.' Attachment and relationship are integral to God.

What does it mean when we say that humankind is made in the image of God? Surely not that God has a head and a body, hands and eyes! Surely to be made in the image of God means more than this. It must mean that we resemble God in the most basic 'movements' known to us — and this includes the experience of our sexuality. Our sexuality resembles the nature of God. Our core desire is to be like God. Thereby, God can be seen as both masculine and feminine.

Earlier, I mentioned that one of the keys to human wholeness is a preparedness on our parts to integrate positive feminine and masculine traits within our psyches. We should recognise, as Jung pointed out, that we have the potential to tease opposite sex characteristics up from our unconscious. Not that we should all become androgynous beings — far from it. Men will still be men and women women, but we are also likely to be more balanced human beings if we recognise our opposite sex traits and foster them in healthy ways.

We are also likely to have a greater appreciation of the opposite sex if we see hints of the other within ourselves. Frederick Buechner, the Pulitzer Prize-nominated author and Christian thinker has said: 'There is a female element in every male just as there is a male element in every female, and most people if they're honest will acknowledge having been at one time or another attracted to both.'[1]

And yet this is a big ask for some people. Many do everything they can to suppress the *anima* or the *animus* when they appear from the unconscious. Interesting isn't it, that the church seems to have done the same to God? We have made him into an *animus* God: competitive, aloof, aggressive. And while I don't disagree that God certainly exhibits such characteristics, I wonder where our *anima* God has gone: the intuitive, nurturing, compassionate, relational Being who doesn't fix or solve everything.

Why is it that when our car won't start in the morning we blame God for not getting the engine to kick over, rather than sensing that God is waiting patiently for the mobile mechanic beside us? Because we've only ever been seduced by a masculine God and have not allowed the feminine face of God to emerge fully.

I understand the great concerns many people have about acknowledging a feminine side to God's nature.

They fear that we might be drifting back into the destructive pagan religions that worshipped the Mother Goddess. The Greeks called her Artemis and the Syrians, Atargatis. The Egyptians worshipped her as Isis and the Assyrians as Ishtar. In Jeremiah's day, the women kneaded dough to make cakes in her likeness and burned incense to her. She is the goddess of heaven and earth who answers petitions, who represents the unbridled, vital force of natural life and who assures us of the unceasing fertility of the earth. But for many, the cost of such fertility was great, indeed.

To worship them meant to accept the supremacy of nature. This meant that sexuality was at the centre of life and that sexual rites were an important part of religious observance. For the most part, these religious rites involved sacred prostitution. Martin Buber, the German theologian, claims that one of the greatest threats to a healthy, integrated faith in God is from the pagan mother goddess cult. He believes it threatens the humanity of women, because it is a religious outlook that worships the force of fertility, the force that creates life.

When we begin to think that the creation of life is a divine force itself, worthy of our worship, we begin to see women exclusively as only fulfilling a sexual role. Women are objects through which the divine force of fertility works, not subjects made in the image of God and valuable inherently beyond their wombs and breasts.

As Paul D. Hanson, a Christian writer, says of the cult of the mother goddess in Babylon: 'Though the dominant metaphor in this cult is feminism, it is dedicated to the view of woman which reduces her to a sex object (as the fertility plaques with their exaggerated representations of the breasts and genitalia illustrate), thereby thrusting life into a debased one-dimensionality.'[2]

Even during biblical times, mother goddesses with their fertility cults were a force to be reckoned with. In the book of Acts in the New Testament, Artemis is referred to as 'Diana of the Ephesians'. In Acts 19, she was acclaimed by the crowd in the theatre at a public demonstration against the Christian and Jewish faiths which refused to acknowledge her as the Great Mother, also known as Cybele, who had a strong following in Rome. In Ephesus and other places, St Paul had to struggle against the same debasing naturalistic paganism.

So there is good reason to maintain a certain reservation in speaking of the motherhood of God. But let's not throw the baby out with the bathwater. I mean, we don't abandon masculine language for God just because pagan gods like Zeus and Hermes were men. I don't hear people saying, 'We mustn't refer to God as Father because it could lead to worshipping masculine deities like Ba'al or even Jupiter.' It is legitimate to posit a feminine image for God within the same parameters as orthodox faith has posited a masculine image for him.

✠ The Bible and the feminine face of God

I want us to look to the Bible again in order to discover some more of the ancient wisdom regarding the feminine face of God. Many people are under the impression that the Bible is an intensely sexist book, with very little interest in the status of women — let alone descriptions of God in feminine terms.

I'll grant that the Bible was written in an ancient, patriarchal culture by men, who used masculine language, symbols and ideas when talking about God. And if that was the end of the story, then we'd be able to say with some confidence that the God they describe is just a construct that reflects their social circumstances. In other words, we could conclude that the ancient Jewish and Christian thinkers and writers have just re-created God in their own image. It was Voltaire who captured this concept when he said: 'In the beginning God created man, and man has been returning the favour ever since.'

But that's not the end of the story. The fact that very feminine symbols and ideas about God have crept into the Bible, even though it was written out of a very patriarchal society, is testimony to me that the biblical God is not just the creation of a male-dominated culture. It actually augurs well for the integrity and authenticity of the biblical material.

The notion in the Bible of God's feminine nature includes at least two very clear aspects: first, God births us; and second, he nurtures us.

☐ *Images in the Bible of God birthing us*
It's not a wildly radical idea to think of God as the giver and sustainer of life. I'm not by any means suggesting that these are distinctly feminine roles. However, the biblical writers are quite happy to express these truths in feminine or motherly ways.

The Bible affirms that when God gives life, he does

it as a woman in childbirth. Listen to Psalm 139, verses 13 to 15:

> *You created my inmost being;;*
> *you knit me together in my*
> *mother's womb.*
> *I praise you because I am fearfully*
> *and wonderfully made;*
> *your works are wonderful ----*
> *I know that full well.*
> *My frame was not hidden from you*
> *when I was made in the secret*
> *place.*
> *When I was woven together in the*
> *depths of the earth,*
> *your eyes saw my unformed body.*

Here, the writer of the psalm rehearses the belief that God creates and forms human life *in utero*. I have occasionally shown a film to high school students that depicts exquisitely detailed photography of the development of a child from a single cell to the moment of delivery. After the students have watched nerve endings intertwining in time-lapse photography, it's easy to read a Bible passage like 'you knit me together in my mother's womb'. The psalmist didn't have the benefit of *in utero* camera work, but he had the general idea right. God, like a magnificent cosmic mother, forms us in the womb.

But God does more than fashion us in the womb. He *knows* us in the womb as well. Just as an expectant mother bonds with her unborn child, so God knows us intuitively. Another Old Testament writer, Jeremiah, claims in Jeremiah 1, verse 5 to have heard God say to him:

> *Before I formed you in the womb,*
> *I knew you;*
> *before you were born,*
> *I set you apart.*

Naturally, I have absolutely no conception whatever (no pun intended) of what it must be like to carry another human being within me, to give it life and to birth it into this world. As a mother bonds intimately with her unseen offspring, God knows us even before we are conceived. There is very strong feminine language and symbolism at work here.

In the New Testament, we find Jesus imaging a feminine, motherly role for God, also. In John's Gospel, we find Jesus telling a religious leader named Nicodemus that he must be 'born again'. Now, this phrase seems to have been used as a slogan by presidents and tele-evangelists for decades to the point that it has lost its original intent. Being born again is Jesus' image for the kind of new birth that only God can create in people. Just as we were birthed once quite naturally by our mothers, God can rebirth us spiritually. William James' book *The Varieties of Religious Experiences* (1901) very adequately explored this idea with once-born and twice-born people.

Once-born people, according to James, are those who have never been forced to assess their own level of spirituality. They have grown up adopting their family's views on life and religion and self without much question or personal investment. They tend to believe simplistic, childish formulations about God being in his heaven and everything being right with the world. They expect that bad things will happen to bad people and good things to the good.

Twice-born people are those who have been forced, usually by personal tragedy or disappointment, to confront those simple, optimistic views on life and to rediscover tougher, more resilient, less cheery, more realistic formulations for making sense of their worlds. In fact, even those who have come to reject their family's values or religious faith are still once-born while ever they have not replaced it with something else of their own. This 'second birth' involves the death of your parents' psychological and spiritual hold on you *and* the initiation of a personal genuine faith.

It was this new birth that Nicodemus could not appreciate. In childlike frustration, he asked the all-too-obvious in John 3, verse 4: 'How can a man be born when he is old? Surely, he cannot enter a second time into his mother's womb to be born.' It's a fair question — and Jesus in verse 5 responded as frankly:

> *I tell you the truth, no-one can enter the kingdom of God unless he is born of water and the Spirit. Flesh gives birth to flesh, but the Spirit gives birth to spirit.*

The picture of the Spirit of God birthing the spirit of a man just as a woman births the flesh of a child is powerful imagery. Human birth involves pain, struggle, travail and fear. So, too, does spiritual rebirth. For most of us, being 'born again' involved a long and uncomfortable pregnancy, a protracted and difficult labour and a traumatic birth. That's the way it often is.

Meister Eckhart, the medieval Christian mystic, was noted for saying: 'What does God do all day long? God gives birth. From all eternity, God lies on a maternity bed giving birth.'

☐ *Images in the Bible of God nurturing us*
But God is not only the mother who births us into this chaotic and haphazard world. He is the mother who nurtures and feeds us once we're here. One of my favourite passages in the Old Testament is Isaiah 66, verses 12 and 13. It goes like this:

> *You shall be nursed,*
> *you shall be carried on the hip,*
> *and fondled on the knees.*
> *As one whom his mother comforts,*
> *so I will comfort you.*

The imagery here is very potent. It implies that we, like little children, are suckled by God in the same way children are breastfed by their mothers. To be nursed is a euphemism for being fed at the breast. A wetnurse is a woman who breastfeeds another's child. The Nursing Mothers' Association is an organisation committed to promoting breastfeeding with new mothers. When the Bible says we shall be nursed by God, it means we will be fed by him.

Now as I write this, there has been a celebrated case

reported in the papers where a young couple took their baby to a restaurant, whereupon the mother proceeded to breastfeed her infant at the table. They were invited to leave. Subsequently, they took the restaurant's management to court and won. In some quarters, there is still the stigma of offense attached to feeding a baby at the breast in public. Many churches would consider it offensive for a woman to breastfeed in the pews.

Shortly after this restaurant episode, it was reported in the print media that a young woman was ejected from a local law court for breastfeeding. It's a very powerful image, the idea of a child being sustained at its mother's breast. I guess that's because a woman's breast is a very stimulating image in a male-dominated society.

Well, here we have the Bible daring to suggest that we, as infants, are sustained at God's breast. That's a very sexually explosive image for a start. It's bold enough to suggest a very feminine role being played by God who is often thought of in male terms.

Does God have breasts? Of course not. God is a spirit. He doesn't have breasts any more than he has eyes or hands. But we're very comfortable talking about God's eyes being upon us or his hands being swift to help us. We recognise that the image is metaphorical. So is the metaphor of God's breasts, but it's a metaphor we seem more ready to forget. Said St Teresa of Avila: 'For from those divine breasts where it seems God is always sustaining the soul, there flow streams of milk bringing comfort to all the people.'

But further to this, the passage in Isaiah 66 outlines the picture of a woman carrying her child on her hip or jostling a baby on her knee. There is a delightful sense of tenderness and nurture associated with this idea. God breastfeeds us, God carries us on his hip and bounces us on his knee. And God comforts us the way our mothers comforted us on our sickbeds or after some trauma or tragedy of one kind or another. Isaiah 66 clearly tells us that God comforts the way a mother comforts her offspring: with tenderness and intuition, with compassion and patience.

Prior to this most explosive passage, the prophet Isaiah had already built up the idea of a feminine, motherly God. Back in chapter 46, verse 15 he says that God is an even better mother than the best mother imaginable:

Can a mother forget her infant,
or be without tenderness for the child of her womb?
Even should she forget,
I will never forget you.

Even when the most perfect mother has forgotten her child, God will continue to remember his children. But it doesn't end with childhood. Isaiah 46, verse 4 says God nurtures us throughout our lives:

Even to your old age I am the same,
even when your hair is grey I will bear you;
It is I who have done this, I who will continue,
and I who will carry you to safety.

This takes us back to old Nicodemus' question regarding rebirth as a mature person. Not only can God birth us as older people; he can carry us on his hip and bounce us on his knee as older people, also.

Perhaps the most consistent image in the Old Testament that carries with it allusions of God's femininity is that of the female eagle. Virginia Mollenkott in her book, *The Divine Feminine*, suggests that the references to God as an eagle in the Old Testament peculiarly imply a *female* eagle.

Those of us who have had to be content with a Western masculine reading of the Bible have often assumed the eagle referred to in such passages as 'May you receive a full reward from the Lord, the God of Israel, under whose wings you have come for refuge' and 'In the shadow of your wings I take refuge, till harm pass by' is the strong, powerful male eagle — like the dominant symbol of the American eagle. But Mollenkott believes that students of eagle behaviour insist that the wings referred to in the Bible belong to the mother eagle.

Sadly, certain English translations of the Bible have referred to the eagle image for God either in the masculine or even the neuter. Even a passage as obviously feminine as Deuteronomy 32 has been translated as though the eagle is a *thing*! However, listen to it in the feminine: '. . .like an eagle that stirs up her nest and hovers over her young, that spreads her wings to catch them and carries them on her pinions'. The image of God being like a mother eagle, stirring her young from the nest, but always being there to support them and catch them, is a tender illustration of God's feminine side. The masculine eagle vigilantly protects and guards the nest and the female eagle hovers over her brood with motherly care. God is clearly illustrated by both images.

George Adam Smith, the well-known Scottish theologian, writing at the end of the last century before feminism became a force, interpreted a similar passage in Isaiah 31 as a strong affirmation of the motherhood of God. He referred to 'a motherhood of pity in the breast of God' and said that, since all fullness dwells in God himself, 'not only may we rejoice in that pity and wise provision for our wants, in that pardon and generosity which we associate with the name of father, but also in the wakefulness, the patience, the love, lovelier with fear, which makes a mother's heart so dear and indispensable'.[3]

So, when we see the feminine qualities of God expressed in the Bible and by theologians, we must surely recognise that this is not to be put down to some subversive, modernist feminist plot. These are the words of scripture. God is mother as he is father.

✠ Paul Smith and feminine roles of God

Paul Smith, a Southern Baptist preacher from Missouri, has written an incisive book on this issue called, *Is It Okay To Call God 'Mother'?* He outlines a number of metaphors or images used in the Bible that explicitly refer to or imply a feminine face of God.

The two major themes outlined above are included as well as the following:

☐ First, God is a seamstress

It might be lost on modern readers, but the woman of the house was specifically responsible for clothing the family. The role of seamstress was hers and hers alone. In a day and age where men think little of washing, ironing or buying their own clothes, we might have difficulty recognising the gravity of some of the biblical material that recalls God as the 'clother' of his people. In Genesis 3, there is the almost throwaway line that God himself made garments from animal skin to clothe man and woman. The same allusion occurs in the story of Job 10, verses 10 to 12.

Even more explicitly in the New Testament, Jesus refers to God the seamstress in Luke's Gospel. Speaking of the futility of worrying in chapter 12, verses 27 and 28, he says:

> *Consider how the lilies grow. They do not labour or spin. Yet I tell you, not even Solomon in all his splendour was dressed like one of these. If that is how God clothes the grass of the field, which is here today and tomorrow is thrown into the fire, how much more will he clothe you?*

Again, I need to stress that this was a peculiarly feminine role. Men simply had nothing to do with the production or maintenance of clothing.

❏ *Second, God is a midwife*

This is another potent image. As if God the birthing mother is not graphic enough, in Psalm 22, verse 9, he is portrayed as the assistant at the birth: 'You brought me out of the womb; you made me trust in you even at my mother's breast.'

The only assistants at birth in biblical times were female members of the expectant mother's family.

Again, the imagery is somewhat lost on modern readers. Today, most obstetricians are men. In fact, many nurses are men. And, of course, expectant fathers are encouraged to stay in the delivery ward and assist in the birth.

An elderly friend of mine tells me that whenever his wife went into labour, he would drop her off at the hospital and go play golf, calling for a report after the first nine! In ancient times, only mothers and aunts and grandmothers were in attendance. The one whose hands eased the new-born infant from the birth canal and placed it at its mother's breast was *always* a woman.

Here, the psalmist dares to ascribe such a role metaphorically to God.

☐ *Third, God is a fierce mother bear*
In Hosea 13, verses 6 to 8, there is an intriguing and powerfully visual image of God's protective mother-love. The Bible here refers to God as a female wild animal:

> So I will come upon them like a lion;
> like a leopard, I will lurk by the path.
> Like a bear robbed of her cubs,
> I will attack them and rip them open.
> Like a lion I will devour them;
> a wild animal will tear them apart.

Now, only the gender of the bear is mentioned, but it seems apparent that we might just as well be talking about the mother lion or leopard. The imagery of the powerful, uncompromising savagery of the protective mother bear is a fascinating illustration of God's swift expression of anger. It's a well-known fact today, as then, that the wild mother animal when protecting her young is a lethal prospect. In Hosea's language, the motherly quality of savage protection can equally be applied to God.

☐ *Fourth, God is a mother with her weaned child*
This image takes further the ideas of birthing and nurturing at the breast. It indicates that even after the frantic period following a new birth, when a mother becomes at ease with her infant and the child with its mother, in that sense of contentment there is a hint of our relationship with God. Read Psalm 131:

> My heart is not proud, O Lord,
>   my eyes are not haughty;
> I do not concern myself with great matters
>   or things too wonderful for me.
> But I have stilled or quieted my soul;
>   like a weaned child with its mother,
> like a weaned child is my soul within me.

The desperate cries of a new-born infant squealing for the breast seem to be a time of great panic. The child has no patience, no notion of waiting. It desires to be gratified immediately. But the psalmist suggests there is a time when the weaned child can relax and abide in its mother's presence. Young children can melt into their mothers' arms and enjoy the embrace for long periods of time. The writer of this psalm yearns for a similar relationship with God, a relationship where there is stillness and contentment.

Further to this, he yearns for a relationship where all the answers need not be forthcoming. He is content to abandon all the so-called important questions of life and simply abide in his mother's presence.

Do you recall that I suggested it's invariably our fathers who have to answer all the dilemmas and solve all the conundrums of our lives? Mothers can tolerate not knowing, not solving. This psalm is a beautifully scripted cry for intimacy without answers, for a mother's kind of love.

Jesus mentioned something similar when he called a little child to stand among his disciples and told them that they, if they wished to be great, must become like a child. In fact, he went so far as to suggest that, unless we become like little children, we will never enter the kingdom of heaven.

I realise that he wasn't referring to God's motherly qualities in Matthew 18, but he was, I believe, hinting at the same wonderful sense of security that children have in their parents, without having to fathom matters 'too wonderful for me'. It's in our mothers' arms that we often experience such contentment.

✠ The image of God as a woman

So far, we have observed God's feminine nature as being very motherly in its biblical form. The ideas of birthing and nurture are traditionally mothering roles. But God is also presented in the Old Testament as a beautiful, mature woman. It is the powerful, feminine image of God known to the Hebrew people as 'Wisdom'.

In fact, in the Hebrew language, 'wisdom' is a

feminine noun. It is Wisdom that is personified as an intelligent, magnificent woman. Proverbs 8, verse 11 says: 'For Wisdom is more precious than rubies, and nothing you desire can compare with her.' And in the Hebrew's Book of Wisdom 7, verse 29, it adds: 'For she [Wisdom] is fairer than the sun, and surpasses every constellation of the stars.' In fact, as Proverbs 8 continues, Wisdom is not only wildly beautiful; she is God's playful mate. Remember, there is only one God. What the Hebrews envisioned was an aspect to God's nature that, like a female companion, supported his creative work in this world. In verses 27 to 29, Wisdom says:

> I was there when he set the heavens
> in place,
> when he marked out the horizon
> on the face of the deep,
> when he gave the sea its boundary
> so the waters would not overstep his command,
> and when he marked out the foundations of the earth.

So far so good. But what was Wisdom doing while God was at work? Verse 30 tells us:

> I was by his side, a master craftsman,
> delighting him, day after day,
> ever at play in his presence.

How delightful! Here is God, the playful young woman. But Wisdom is more than a bystander. She is an image of the invisible God, an important aspect of the divine nature. The Book of Wisdom is not accepted widely as a part of the Bible, though it appears in many versions as what is known as an apocryphal book. The aspect of God's femininity appears quite explicitly in some passages of this work, including chapter 7, verses 22b and 23:

For in her is a spirit,
  intelligent, holy, unique,
Manifold, subtle, agile,
  clear, unstained, certain.
Not baneful, loving the good, keen,
  unhampered, beneficent, kindly,
Firm, secure, tranquil,
  all-powerful, all-seeing,
And pervading all spirits,
  though they be intelligent, pure and very subtle.

Here the femininity of God, as personified by Wisdom, appears as a wise, mature, righteous woman.

She is a breath of the power of God,
  pure emanation of the glory of the Almighty;
  hence nothing impure can find a way into her.
She is a reflection of the eternal light,
  untarnished mirror of God's active power,
  image of his goodness.

There's no question that the biblical writers were much more relaxed about embracing the feminine aspects to God's character than we are today. It seems that over the generations we have either forgotten or ignored — or even retranslated — passages that point up both sides of God's sexual nature.

✠ Our need to come to terms with God's femininity

It would seem apparent that we have done to God what we do to ourselves. Just as we foster the *animus* or *anima*, depending on our gender, and subjugate the other within our unconscious, we seem to have suppressed God's *anima*, allowing only his so-called masculine traits to be perceived.

The church has cultivated this one-sided God — or, should I say, the male leadership of the church throughout the centuries has cultivated such a view of God for, until recently, women had little say in biblical translation and theological debate. But as we saw from the beginning, the most honest way to encounter truth is through paradox. The paradoxical nature of God's sexual idenitity has been abandoned by a church that has been timid about matters of sexuality at the best of times.

Surely, it's now time to recognise both sides of God's nature: the transcendent and the immanent, the masculine and the feminine. It seems the time is right to look squarely into the feminine face of God.

I know that when I speak this way about God, even though I can demonstrate that the biblical writers did so, it causes some Christians a degree of consternation. I have been accused of a feminist form of anthropomorphism — that is, creating God in the likeness of a woman. God is *not* a woman, I have been forcefully told — and I agree. God is neither male nor female. God is spirit and therefore has no gender.

So why then has it been so acceptable throughout the centuries to speak of God in distinctly male terms?

In many cases, male language, male images and male characteristics have been explicitly associated with our idea of God. It begs the question as to why this kind of anthropomorphism is so acceptable, when the use of feminine terminology is such a scandal.

There is simply no justification for this bias. Either we can speak of God in terms that humans can relate to — which includes language and allusions of an anthropomorphic kind — or we can't. And if we can't, we must be just as prepared to stop speaking of God in masculine terms as in feminine terms.

Such a course of action would be considered silly. We can only speak of an Ultimate Being like God in terms that make sense to us. We know God no more has breasts than he has eyes. Why is the former considered offensive while the latter is helpful? I think it's more revealing of our prejudice against the female body in contrast to the male body. You can't help but wonder whether the image of God with breasts may seem unacceptable because of our misguided association of female sexual characteristics with evil, seduction or inferiority. It says rather more about the way we see ourselves than it does about our view of God.

Having said all of this, I am not wanting to suggest that we make the issue of God's breasts some theological battleground. This is not the issue. He doesn't have breasts because he doesn't have a body. But surely the image of the breast is one of nurture, comfort and sustenance, qualities we can most certainly attribute to God. This imagery surely is no different from that of the hand as an image of assistance and support and friendship, also qualities we apply to the divine.

All analogies and metaphors, without exception, say something that is false, even as they're saying something that is true. The Bible affirms that 'God is a consuming fire' and 'God is our Father'. Neither metaphor says everything there is to say about God and, taken alone, they can suggest inaccurate things about God. More than one word picture is needed to get a balanced understanding.

It's not only biblical writers who were brave enough to recognise anthropomorphic language for what it is. Throughout the history of the Christian church, there have been notable voices calling the majority back to this sense of balance, recognising God's masculine movements and his feminine, affirming God's motherhood and fatherhood. Virginia Mollenkot lists St John Chrysostom, Gregory of Nyssa, the Venerable Bede, Thomas Aquinas, Bonaventure, Bernard of Clairvaux and Anselm of Canterbury — among many others.

In fact, St Anselm wrote a prayer in the eleventh century which became widely known and in which the divine motherhood was the central idea. He took his lead from a passage in Galatians in the New Testament in which Paul says of his Christian friends, 'my little children, with whom I am again in travail until Christ be formed in you'.

This impressed St Anselm so greatly that he constructed a prayer to Paul, in which he addressed him as 'my sweet nurse, sweet mother'. Addressing prayers to saints is not a practice I would encourage, but to call the apostle Paul your *mother* is really saying something! But he goes on to address Jesus: 'And you, Jesus, are you not also a mother? Are you not the mother who like a hen gathers her children under wings?. . . Then, both of you are mothers. Even if you are fathers, you are also mothers. . . Fathers by your authority, mothers by your kindness; fathers by your teaching, mothers by your mercy.'

How delightful that in the eleventh century the movements of human sexuality that we consider we are just beginning to formulate were *already* clear and being attributed to the divine. There is no question that in both Jewish and Christian literature over the centuries the feminine movements of God have been embraced as helpful metaphors for understanding God and his inter-action with humankind.

The high water mark for this understanding was in the person of Christ who, though human, modelled complete sexual integration in the same manner as God.

8

JESUS AND SEXUALITY

What a well-integrated personality looks like

O, what is this? But our true Mother Jesus; he alone bears us for joy and for endless life; blessed may he be. So he carries us within him in love and travail, until the full time when he wanted to suffer the sharpest thorns and cruel pains that ever were or will be, and at the last he died.

Julian of Norwich

'This man' has not been a failure yet, for nobody has ever been sane enough to try his way.

George Bernard Shaw

WHEN I WAS A TEENAGER, I REMEMBER SEEING a film that took my breath away. It was called the *Poseidon Adventure* and it was to become the first of a long series of disaster films in the 'seventies. The basic plot concerned an ocean liner, like the QE II or some similarly opulent passenger liner, filled with an assortment of world travellers, being hit by a tidal wave in the middle of the ocean somewhere. But rather than sinking without trace, this ocean liner turns belly up and floats upside down for the rest of the film.

The passengers that survive the dreadful impact of the wave now find themselves standing on the ceiling of the inverted craft. And so begins their remarkable adventure. The first dilemma they must overcome is to be prepared to recognise that the ship is upside down and that the way out is to make it to the bottom of the craft, which is now the top. This is so great a mind shift for many of them that the thought of heading deeper into the belly of the boat cannot be comprehended.

It takes a charismatic and unorthodox Christian minister, played by Gene Hackman, to convince some of them that heading to the bottom of the ship is the way to salvation. He rants and raves, bullies and cajoles them into recognising that everything is the wrong way up. 'We must head *down* the ship if we want to get *up* to the surface,' he pleads. Few of them, in their dazed confusion, can grasp what he is telling them. Finally, his strength of character and his dramatic presentation of the facts convinces a handful of the survivors to follow him up to the hull of the liner.

There is another minister, a Catholic priest, among the survivors. He is moving around the crowd, offering comfort and solace in the midst of turmoil and pain. Gene Hackman's character appeals to him to join his group on the journey to salvation. The priest agrees with the minister that indeed what he is suggesting is true. The priest admits that the way out is by doing the opposite of what you would normally want to do. 'But,' says the priest, 'I will not come with you. These people need me here. I will stay with them, offering them comfort in the midst of their lostness.'

These two men model the two major movements of human sexuality. One is concerned with penetrating deeper into the ship. The other is concerned with enveloping and nurturing. The fact that they are both Christian ministers got me thinking. Christian ministry is meant to be a life lived in imitation of Christ. So it occurred to me that these two characters, basing their lives on Jesus, were actually modelling different things.

Was Jesus both of these things? Certainly he was. In a very clear sense, Jesus was both masculine and feminine. Like Gene Hackman's character, he was charismatic and dynamic. He called upon people to follow him. He had to redirect people's attention and get them to think in ways they were not used to thinking. He was interested in penetrating structures. He was complete, effective and controlling. But he was also like the Catholic priest. He was concerned with nurturing the lost, comforting the oppressed and offering solace to the helpless. Never has one individual so exquisitely integrated both sexual archetypes so successfully.

Jesus really is an enigma to many people and his sexuality is considered to be even more mysterious. When, in the rock opera *Jesus Christ Superstar*, Mary Magdalene sings, 'I Don't Know How To Love Him', she expresses the general frustration we all seem to experience regarding our view of Jesus. We're uncertain of how to — or whether to — view him as a sexual being.

Many portraits or pictorial representations of Jesus present him as looking very feminine. His features are usually soft, his eyes are gentle and pretty and his hair is neatly coiffed. Some portrayals, such as *Christa*, the well-known sculpture of a naked female messiah hanging on a cross, are explicit in their expression of his femininity. I think part of the reason for this is that we recognise that Jesus was unlike any other human being. He was a man, but how do we portray a man who is like no other? Portray him as looking (but never being) feminine!

This inability to even come close to an appreciation of Jesus' sexuality is reflected in the church's coyness about his body and in particular his genitals. You see, even though it's true that Jesus died naked on the cross (as every other crucified criminal died), you never see a crucified image of him without clothing. I'm sure the church was being very zealous when it took this line, perhaps thinking it was 'impure' and would corrupt those viewers who looked upon the messiah's private parts, but it wasn't very accurate. Like most people, even today, the thought police of the church were afraid of nakedness.

Nakedness for human beings involves humility and embarrassment. Those Jews who were herded into the showers at Buchenwald and Auschwitz to be exterminated were naked, their humiliation complete. Jesus' humiliation was also complete as he, without a stitch of clothing, was forced to watch Roman soldiers gamble for his robe.

But nakedness is also powerful. It can also be an expression of personal dignity. Our nakedness can be about our preparedness to just be ourselves without the veneer of clothing to make us 'someone'. Jesus died with this sense of power and dignity. Remember, it's always about a paradox! It's important to realise that Jesus didn't die as a naked nobody, but as a naked somebody, because he was loving us with the kind of love that lovers know. And I think there is even more to it than that. Let's look at both the masculine and feminine movements apparent in Jesus' short life.

✠ The masculinity of Jesus

When we say Jesus was masculine, we must be referring to much more than that he was rough and tough and muscular and was possessed of male genitalia. I have seen some dreadful Marvel comic versions of Gospel stories where Jesus looks like a classic superhero, like Captain America or Spiderman, with muscles rippling. A friend of mine wonders whether Arnold Schwarzeneggar *could* play Jesus in a film version of the Easter story. He imagines Jesus the Terminator hanging on the cross and uttering the words, with an Austrian accent, 'I'll be *back!*'

Nonetheless, Jesus' dramatic death and his remarkable resurrection, not to mention many other aspects of his life and teaching, reflect some distinctly masculine movements. And this has been a theme in Christian thinking since the first days of the church. Jesus is correctly portrayed as an effective, successful victor over the forces of evil.

In Matthew's Gospel, just after Jesus entered Jerusalem for the last time, two interesting events occur that demonstrate Jesus' quick, effective, masculine control.

❑ *First, Jesus' masculinity is revealed in the events just before his death*

In Matthew 21, verses 12 and 13, Jesus enters the Temple in Jerusalem, the international centre of Jewish worship, only to discover that it was filled, not only with worshippers, but with opportunists making a quick buck out of the religious devotion of the faithful. There were money-changers and dealers cheating the interstate and overseas worshippers with excessive rates of exchange and by the exhorbitant price of animals and doves necessary for sacrifice.

Jesus, filled with outrage that something as pure and righteous as worship could be the source of fortune for heartless opportunists, turns their tables over and takes a whip to the scoundrels. He could see that Jewish worship had become so commercialised, and regarded so much as an end in itself, that it was merely a shadow of what it had intended to represent — God's relationship with his people. Jesus takes matters into his own hands and drives the money-changers and salesmen out of the Temple precincts. He is rough, uncompromising, controlling and effective.

Mind you, it is still controlled anger. Contrary to the usual pictures in children's Bibles which show doves flying in all directions, thoughtful commentators have noted that it was the tables of *money* that were upended, not the tables carrying the birds. Jesus was protective of them.

Then Matthew records another instance where Jesus surprised those around him with a dashing display of masculine power. He had left Jerusalem again to spend the night in the rural township of Bethany just outside the city: 'Early in the morning, as he was on his way back to the city, he was hungry. Seeing a figtree by the road, he went up to it but found nothing on it except leaves. Then he said to it, "May you never bear fruit again!" Immediately, the tree withered.'

At first, this looks like a dreadful fit of pique, as the

messiah does his block on a fruitless tree, but there's more to it than first meets the eye. Apparently, some figs usually appear on a fig tree *before* the leaves, when a tree was in full leaf. Those who approach it would naturally expect to find it bearing a crop.

Imagine Jesus' disappointment when, feeling peckish before breakfast, he sees a tree in full leaf only to discover it barren of fruit! Such a fruitless tree, though seemingly alive, was in fact dying. Jesus again takes matters into his own hands and foretells of its imminent destruction. This is no divine temper tantrum. He has taken control and put the sickly tree out of its misery in a very masculine way.

There's even more to each of these stories than just a reminder of Jesus' masculinity. They are each symbolic of an even greater truth. The driving of businessmen out of the Temple is symbolic of Jesus' denunciation of the emptiness of Jewish worship. And the withering of the fig tree is symbolic of the fruitlessness of Israel's faith.

The Jewish nation held out before the world such promise that it was spiritually rich in fruit, but it was being rendered barren by empty legalism and ceremonialism. Jesus' destruction of the tree symbolised the future of a fruitless Israel. In each of these cases, Jesus indicated his position with swift, uncompromising control. He would not tolerate the situation any further. They had to be dealt with now. And deal with them he does.

The Gospel of John records one more telling incident, showing Jesus' raw courage. The religious hierarchy were tired of playing ducks and drakes with

Jesus over the question of his messiahship. Confronting him in mid-winter in the Temple precincts, they tackled him: 'How long will you keep us in suspense? If you are the Messiah, tell us plainly' (John 10, verse 24, NRSV).

Now a lynch squad is a very unpleasant sight at the best of times. Death by stoning was a particularly gruesome and humiliating death. When the religious leaders took up stones, Jesus answered his accusers calmly and rationally — and then, when they tried to arrest him, just walked away! Another passage says he just walked through the midst of the hostile crowd.

This took raw physical courage and incredible personal power — masculine power, if you will.

☐ *Second, Jesus' masculinity is revealed in his death*
While I realise that crucifixion on a hill between two thieves is not exactly the sort of 'success' characteristic of maleness, his ultimate vindication on Easter Sunday is a triumph, a victory standard. The idea of challenging the darkness, defeating pretenders to his throne, triumphing single-handedly and completing the assigned task echo many of the ultimate concerns of men. All this makes up the church's doctrine of atonement and Jesus comes out of this doctrine looking very masculine. We need to carefully reexamine this idea of atonement briefly.

The doctrine of atonement has been one of the core beliefs in Christianity from its inception. But it was best and most dramatically expressed by the reformer Martin Luther. In his writings, the atonement was portrayed as a divine conflict and victory.

Martin Luther loved violent expressions, strong colours and realistic images and so naturally in many of his writings he describes the ministry of Jesus in this way. As Gustaf Aulen once said: 'For him [Luther] no colours are too strong, no images too concrete. . . Luther seems to have a special fondness for the grossest symbols of all.'[1] When explaining the atonement, he does so with particular relish.

To atone for something is to perform some action that brings mutual reconciliation between estranged people. A very inadequate illustration might be the way we pay a speeding fine to bring ourselves and the police department back to even terms. At a more complex level, it refers to the 'payment' individuals might make in order to guarantee reconciliation. The doctrine of atonement is similar. It holds that humans and God were irreconcilably separated by the sin of humankind.

God is perfect and humans are not — that's obvious. But for God to have any contact with us would be to compromise his purity. After all, if you drop a mere modicum of polluted water into a glass of pure water you contaminate the whole glass. The idea of the atonement is that if God was to make contact with humans, he would be contaminated and his perfection compromised. God, motivated by his unending love for humankind, determined to perform some action that would bring about reconciliation. The Christian church believes that that action was the sacrifice of God's human manifestation, Jesus, as an example of vicarious suffering on the part of all humankind.

In other words, Jesus' death and resurrection defeats the forces of sin and death in this world and frees human beings to live up to their potential as individuals created in the image of God. It's a complex doctrine, even though I've just sketched it so briefly. By dying on behalf of sinful humans, Jesus appeases God's refusal to become intimate with imperfect beings.

But the crux is that an atoning sacrifice had to be offered. This idea is common to many religions; the idea that a sacrifice must be offered to atone for the sins of the people. In the Old Testament, sheep and goats and grain offerings were regularly sacrificed to God. In pagan religions, it was virgins or first-born sons. The Christian church believes that the sacrifice of Jesus was enough to cover all humankind once and for all.

The idea of atonement is powerfully explored in a film called *Flatliners*. In this motion picture, several medical students begin to experiment with near-death experiences in order to find out what is on the other side of this life. Each of them agrees to allow the others clinically to stop their heart from beating (hence the title, when the flat line appears on the heart monitor) in order to approach the state beyond death.

In each case (and each successive student dares to have their heart stopped for longer periods), they encounter the 'unfinished business' of their lives. Every student has some 'sin' in their experience for which they have not atoned. Every character in the film has to endure some form of suffering in order to be freed from the effects of their misdemeanour. In some cases, the ordeal through which they go is traumatic and extremely painful. The under-lying conviction which provides the framework for the film is that we all need to atone for our past mistakes.

This is a fundamentally Christian conviction.

In the doctrine of atonement, Jesus is the atoning sacrifice for all our past mistakes. His death frees us from the forces that retard our potential and hold us in their sway. His death is a potent symbol of the way to real life. If I can return to the illustration with which I began this chapter, *The Poseidon Adventure*, the very masculine symbol of Jesus played by Gene Hackman ultimately offers himself as an atoning sacrifice in order to free his band of followers.

If you've seen the film, you'll know that when they finally reach the bottom of the liner they discover that the steel floor of the hull stops them from reaching the outer edge of the ship. The only way to get through is by opening a valve door, whose handle is suspended over a burning oil slick. Hackman's character, having led them through innumerable dangers and sustained them by his vision, leaps through the air, takes hold of the handle and, dangling over the flames, opens the hatch to free the others. They can easily scramble through the small doorway, but he cannot make it back to the platform. Having led them to salvation, he can do nothing but allow himself to drop into the fire below.

His sacrifice was like an atonement of sorts. His death was the price of their freedom. You might never have realised it, but the daddy of all disaster films is in fact a Christian parable. But there's more. Recall that I mentioned how Gene Hackman's character modelled a very masculine aspect to Jesus' character. Well, the way the great Christian thinkers have expressed the doctrine of atonement has been in very masculine terms also.

To Martin Luther, the idea of the atonement is always couched in dramatic, violent and competitive terms. For Luther, the atonement was about Jesus defeating the devil. The atoning work of Jesus is powerfully expressed as his conflict with the tyrants of hell. As Gene Hackman defeats the ship, Jesus defeats Satan on the cross and is vindicated through his resurrection.

Luther even uses a classic male illustration: fishing! He speaks of God acting like a fisherman, who binds a line to a fishing rod, attaches a sharp hook, fixes on it a worm and casts it into the water. The fish comes, sees the worm but not the hook and bites, thinking he's got himself a tasty morsel; but the hook is jagged within his mouth and he's caught. The imagery speaks of a God who sends Christ into the world, where the devil finds him like a worm and swallows him up. But Luther goes on: 'Christ sticks in his gills and he must spew him out again, as the whale, the prophet Jonah and, even as he chews him, the devil chokes himself and is slain and is taken captive by Christ.'[2]

There's no question that Martin Luther had a predilection for colourful language, but his 'rediscovery' of the doctrine of the atonement in and around 1515 has set the tone for Protestant thinking ever since. A strong feature of this doctrine is that Jesus is the champion, the winner — the triumphant, conquering (and very masculine) king.

For Luther, the whole crux of the atonement rested on the use of the term 'Lord' when used with reference to Christ. Naturally, 'Lord' is a masculine term, but we won't make too much of this. Nevertheless, the way he uses the term strikes at what I've been saying about the masculine interest in completion, mastery and achievement. Listen further to Luther and recognise that though not too many Christian ministers speak quite so dramatically these days, this theme is still the essence of contemporary Christian doctrine:

> *What is it now to be a 'Lord'? It is this, that he redeemed me from sin, from the devil, from death and all woe. For before, I had not yet had any Lord, nor King, but had been held captive under the devil's power, doomed to death, ensnared in sin and blindness. . . Now, therefore, those tyrants and jailers are all crushed, and in their place is come Jesus Christ, a Lord of Life, righteousness, all good and holiness, and he has snatched us poor lost men from the jaws of hell, won us, made us free, and brought us back to the Father's goodness and grace.*[3]

Time and again, Luther and the other reformers speak of Christ 'overcoming', 'destroying', 'smiting', 'annihilating', 'triumphing', having 'dominion' and 'victory'. It's not just that the language is strongly masculine: the allusions are equally so. In fact, the dramatic, hyperbolic flavour of this language sounds similar to a sports column in a daily newspaper. The reformers — Luther, Calvin and their like — were enamoured of the powerful masculine imagery associated with Christ's work.

For it is fundamental to understanding our Christian heritage that we recognise the degree to which Jesus, in a very masculine fashion, completed the work he set out to achieve. There is very strong evidence in the Gospels that Jesus was single-minded in his commitment to get to Jerusalem, the 'belly of the beast', where he knew forces beyond his control (Luther would say the forces of the devil) were to destroy him.

For example, many Christian thinkers believe that the Gospel of Mark reaches its first climax in chapter 8, verses 31 and 32: '[Jesus] then began to teach them that [he] must suffer many things and be rejected by the elders, chief priests and teachers of the law, and that he must be killed and after three days rise again. He spoke plainly about this. . .'

After this statement, the Gospel picks up speed like a runaway train as Jesus heads resolutely toward the cross. His sacrifice on the cross is the symbol of supreme sacrifice. The cross is an emblem of hard work, courage and sacrifice. But it is also a symbol of completion and mastery. Like the hook at the end of the line, the cross is also an emblem of the ultimate and surprising victory of good over evil. Jesus *does* win in the end.

Like the goodie in the movies who is seemingly vanquished, he rises in the final reel to overcome the baddies. Why do you think so many westerns and science fiction movies have this theme? The marshall in the white hat always comes back from the brink of defeat to triumph over the forces of evil, whether it be Gary Cooper or Kevin Costner, Luke Skywalker or Buffalo Bill. He is the Christ figure. He is the perfect male stereotype — committed, hard working, courageous, honest, triumphant, complete, vindicated.

Movies are reminders to us of ultimate truths; they reinforce longings held by the majority. We yearn for a male role model. Jesus is that template. And all pretenders to that mantle are merely shadows of his example.

✠ The humanity, not the maleness of Jesus is of paramount importance

Some feminist writers claim that this is the very limitation of Jesus that disturbs them most: he is male. They ask, 'Can a male saviour save women?' Since God saw fit to reveal himself through a male saviour, they argue, hasn't he therefore failed to transcend the male/female duality? Isn't he playing favourites?

Says feminist theologian Mary Paterson Corrington: 'Thus the female is rigidly excluded from the personae of the deity and, at the same time, femaleness is devalued as an appropriate personal attribute of the deity.'[4] In other words, God cannot be a God for women while ever he prefers a male saviour.

Personally, I think this is going too far, though I appreciate the frustration many women experience with exclusively masculine deities that has given rise to such a view. To identify Jesus with maleness is to miss the point of Jesus' significance and mission. It would be like identifying him exclusively with Jewishness, living in the first century or being a craftsperson and so forth.

Jesus became flesh to show the love of God. This is not a gooey, romantic show of goodwill, but the kind of tough love of which we spoke in chapter 2, a love which is the heart and cohesive force of the universe. God manifested himself in human form with all the possibilities and limitations of human life. As theologian Patricia Wilson-Kastner says: 'Within this context, Jesus' maleness, like the limited scope of his knowledge, his confinement to the first century in Palestine and various other specifics of this life are all examples of

God's humility and self-emptying in living among us.'[4]

Helpfully, she goes on to summarise that Jesus Christ is the expression of God in *a* human life, not *the* human life. To exalt the particular details of Christ's life as concrete media for the expression of the divine can become ridiculous. Because Christ was male and can only save males, should we claim that because he was a bearded male he can only save bearded males? It's interesting to note that this argument, now being used by feminists, is the very argument used by conservative male theologians against them. We consider it foolishness today to say as they once did that, because Christ was male, only men can perform Christ-like ministry. Why use the same argument to make Jesus obsolete to women? I don't think it holds.

Jesus is not asexual, bisexual or androgynous. He is a perfectly whole human being who models what it looks like when an individual is able to integrate both the masculine and feminine aspects to his personality. It's true that he was born male, but he modelled such a sweet, perfectly balanced type of humanness that we can't but be impressed by his 'femininity' as much as his masculinity. I believe that this male saviour can save women.

And we should make no bones about it — Jesus exhibited clearly masculine characteristics. And he did so in a decidedly positive way. The temptations he endured in the desert prior to beginning his public life represent temptation to wield power in a negative masculine way. Matthew 4, verses 1 to 3 records the first temptation like this: 'Then Jesus was led by the Spirit into the desert to be tempted by the devil. After fasting forty days and forty nights, he was hungry. The tempter came to him and said, "If you are the Son of God, tell these stones to become bread".'

Here, we have a classic instance when Jesus might have abused masculine power over objects for his own ends. There seems to be no inherent condemnation of his ability to control his environment or those around him. Rather, the temptation is to be manipulative or selfish in that capacity to control. But Jesus resists the temptation and allows what many would see as a feminine quality to surface: a deep appreciation of spiritual values. He acknowledges that there are greater values in life than material objects.

On the second temptation, in verses 4 to 6 we read: 'Then the devil took him to the holy city and had him stand on the highest point of the Temple. "If you are the Son of God," he said, "throw yourself down. For it is written: 'He will command his angels concerning you, and they will lift you up in their hands, so that you will not strike your foot against a stone.'"'

You must admit, if Jesus were to have succumbed to such a temptation, it would make a pretty flashy display. Here, in this text, Jesus hears the devil tell him to appear on the highest spire of the holy Temple and to float to the ground suspended by angels and heavenly creatures.

The point made here is that Jesus was being tempted to abuse his power as the Messiah to frighten impressionable people into submitting to him. Many Jews at that time had wild and fantastic expectations about the way that the messiah would finally appear. Simple, uneducated folk are especially vulnerable to the magical;

they follow anyone who can mystify them or fascinate them with the extraordinary.

Jesus is overcome with the temptation to accompany the inauguration of his ministry with a very macho performance. It's a distinctly masculine trait, isn't it? To enjoy and revel in the trappings, the pomp and circumstance of leadership belies the masculine predeliction for accessing reality through objects.

In the third temptation, in verses 8 and 9, Jesus is tempted with political domination: 'Again the devil took him to a very high mountain and showed him all the kingdoms of the world and their splendour. "All this I will give you," he said, "if you will bow down and worship me." How classically masculine is it to hunger after universal control? For centuries, men have fought for political domination, both nationally and internationally. Here, Jesus is presented with the opportunity to use his power to manipulate the world into coming under his control.

Again, he rejects the advances of the devil. Again, he refuses to allow his masculinity to be expressed in detrimental ways. Though decidedly masculine — though capable of controlling his environment, presenting himself dramatically and manipulating those around him for his own ends — Jesus refuses to express his sexuality in a negative way. It is his *animus* held in check by, or perfectly balanced with, his *anima*.

Just as God can only truly be made sense of through the device of paradoxical thinking, Jesus — his human representation on earth — can likewise only be understood paradoxically. He, like God, is both holy and loving, both frightening and comforting, both mysterious and approachable. He perfectly represents the two major movements of human and divine nature. In chapter 4, we looked at God revealing himself to Job and Elijah through the paradox of awe and intimacy.

If that wasn't clear enough, we can look at Jesus as the most exquisite revelation of God's paradoxical nature. Jesus' nature is the perfect synergy of masculinity and femininity, of holiness and love, of awe and intimacy. No wonder he has been so greatly misunderstood throughout history — as he was misunderstood during his lifetime.

There is a wholeness to Jesus' personality. Perfect inner freedom allowed him to respond to people in an appropriate way, depending on the circumstances. So, at times he behaved in a thoroughly masculine way, concerned with control, achievement, mastery as we have seen.

✠ The 'femininity' of Jesus

How astounding that this is the same man who behaved in distinctly feminine ways, also! As we shall now see, Jesus was not only competitive and controlling; he was also concerned with more 'feminine' approaches.

❑ *First, Jesus had an interest in matters thought feminine at the time*

Jesus' interest in connectedness and nurture is clearly demonstrated when he took a young child and had him stand among the big, burly disciples to indicate the power of simplicity. Men were not noted for having anything to do with children. It was considered

women's work to care for or have much at all to do
with little ones. But Jesus' tenderness in calling the
child to him is quite a marked break with tradition.

In fact, his words to his disciples in Matthew 18,
verses 5 to 6 show a tenderness and an interest in
children not common among men at that time: 'Whoever welcomes a little child like this in my name
welcomes me. But if anyone causes one of these little
ones who believe in me to sin, it would be better for
him to have a large millstone hung around his neck and
to be drowned in the depths of the sea.'

The sea, in Jesus' time, was the source of all things
unknowable and frightening. It was believed that dreadful creatures dwelt there. To defend the innocence of a
young child by suggesting that anyone who perverts him
or her should be cast into the sea was tantamount to
suggesting the most cruel death known to man. Remember that we saw God being described as a ferocious mother
bear defending her cubs by one of the Old Testament
writers? Here, we find Jesus behaving in much the same
way. For a single man with no children of his own, this
is a remarkable demonstration of parental tenderness.

Grown Palestinian men also didn't take time to
watch the lillies of the field grow as Jesus did in Matthew
6, verse 28. They didn't stand for a moment on street
corners and watch children at play in the marketplace,
as Jesus did in Matthew 11, verse 16.

☐ *Second, Jesus had a frank and open relationship
with women*

Not only did men in Jesus' time not have anything to

do with children; for the most part, they had nothing to do with women, either. This was a strongly patriarchal society. But Jesus related to women not as a male to females, but almost as a sister.

In *Unpopular Opinions*, writer Dorothy L. Sayers reflects on the ease of the relationship between Jesus and women:

> [Women] had never known a man like this Man --- there never has been such another. A prophet and teacher who never nagged at them, never flattered or coaxed or patronised; who never made arch jokes about them. . . who rebuked without querulousness and praised without condescension. . . who never mapped out their sphere for them, never urged them to be feminine or jeered at them for being female; who had no axe to grind and no uneasy male dignity to defend; who took them as he found them and was completely unselfconscious.[5]

As Sayers points out, Jesus' relatively frank and open relationship with women was quite remarkable. It seems clear that his behaviour towards and treatment of them was well within the bounds of Jewish law. That is to say, even though his friendship with women was extremely unusual, there was no impropriety taking place. If there was, his critics would have been onto him like a shot. He was accused of both drunkenness and gluttony during his life, but never of sexual impropriety. He seems to have been able to walk the fine line of being intimate with women without being improper within the strict Jewish codes of conduct. His attentiveness to women, an astounding feature of his life, was rare within that culture, but never seen as bizarre.

It has been said that what Jesus does *not* do regarding women is almost as remarkable as what he does do. He does not separate women out for special treatment. He does not have some teaching for women and most of it for men. There is never any suggestion that there were two classes of his followers, male and female, and that the males were more important to him. Patricia Wilson-Kastner says: 'Jesus never says anything demeaning to women, trivialises them or praises their special "women's contribution".'⁶

In a famous biblical story, Jesus attends the home of two women, Martha and Mary, and gladly allows Mary to sit at his feet while he teaches her theologically. This was, culturally, a distinctly male position. And yet Jesus behaves as though her position as his disciple was perfectly natural. Not only does he not reject her relationship to him as protégé to mentor; he does not make some big deal about what a radical thing it was to teach a young woman in this way. There is no fuss made about the situation at all. Everything is simple and normal for Jesus. (A fuss is made by Martha because she's doing all the work, while Mary gets to soak up the great teaching, but that's another point.)

Now, something has been made of the fact that Jesus only chose men to be part of his inner circle of twelve disciples. Doesn't this indicate that Jesus wasn't so radical in his acceptance of women after all? some argue.

It's true that Jesus was concerned with cultural sensitivity at this point. As I've indicated, even though his relationship to women was radical, he maintained some semblance of working within the strict cultural expectations of the time. For him to have travelled, eaten, slept and bathed with women as he moved around in his itinerant ministry would have been not just culturally inappropriate, but very near a criminal offence.

In the same way, he didn't invite lepers, Roman soldiers, slaves or children to be numbered among the twelve for clear cultural reasons. But this isn't to say that there are not clear cases of him esteeming and valuing each of these four types of people in the Gospels. His choice of twelve young, able-bodied Jewish men doesn't mean that only people fitting this description are valued by him, either then or today.

❏ *Third, Jesus used feminine imagery of himself*
But it's not only his treatment of women that marks him out as different. It's the way he saw himself that is interesting. There are a number of allusions he makes to his own femininity. The best known of these is in Luke 13, verse 34, where he compares himself to a mother hen gathering her chicks under her wings. It is an image of maternal tenderness.

✠ The integration of masculinity and feminity in Jesus
The juxtaposition of the following in the Gospels well indicate the two sides of Jesus' sexuality.

❏ *First, Jesus demonstrated a strong sense of both attachment and achievement*
In both Luke and Matthew, Jesus speaks in the gentle feminine way indicated above about a mother hen and

her chicks just after using what we might call very masculine language. In Matthew's Gospel, he gives forth with a tirade of scorn and abuse called the Seven Woes, directed at the excesses and false religiosity of Israel, after which he looks to Jerusalem as he says the 'mother hen' words: 'O Jerusalem, Jerusalem. . . how often I have longed to gather your children together, as a hen gathers her chicks under her wings.'

Luke's Gospel records a more brief exchange. Luke recalls the religious leaders, against whom Jesus spoke very forcefully, coming to him to warn him that, if he doesn't shut up, the king, Herod, will have him killed. Jesus' response in verse 32 to this attempted gag is dramatic: 'Go tell that fox, "I will drive out demons and heal people today and tomorrow, and on the third day I will reach my goal."'

This is daring, uncompromising stuff. There is no attempt at conciliation or attachment. He refers to the most powerful man in the land as a 'fox' and basically tells the religious leaders where to go.

After this stinging rebuke, he's drawn to think of the 'goal' to which he is working on that third day — the city of Jerusalem and his own death. It's then that he compares himself with the mother hen. Here is a dramatic instance of both Jesus' masculine and feminine movements coming to the fore. On the one hand, he tells the religious leaders of Jerusalem to get lost because he must reach his goal and, on the other, he yearns to draw all of Jerusalem to his side. Achievement and attachment.

☐ *Second, Jesus identified with*
God's integrated character

In one of his parables, Jesus even dares to compare God to a housewife searching for a single lost coin. This occurs in Luke's Gospel directly before the parable called the Prodigal Son. In that parable, God is compared to a loving father who awaits the return of his wayward son and who, against all cultural expectations, forgives him and reinstates him after he has abandoned the family.

By placing these two stories back-to-back in his Gospel, I believe Luke is clearly indicating the wholeness with which Jesus saw God as both feminine and masculine, as both housewife and father. In John 10, verse 30, Jesus clearly states that he and God are one. As God is an integrated Being, exhibiting qualities we would normally consider to be both masculine and feminine, so does Jesus.

In much the same way that God can reasonably be described as a pregnant woman in labour, bringing forth new life in the midst of travail and trauma, Jesus alludes to himself fulfilling such a role, also. In John 16, verses 22 and 23, he speaks literally of a woman at the onset of labour: 'A woman giving birth to a child has pain because her hour has come. . .' Then shortly after, he says of himself, 'Father, the hour has come.' He is speaking of the hour at which he will be handed over to the religious and civil authorities to be tortured to death, but it is the very same language he uses of the onset of childbirth. Like a mother sensing with some anxiety the first birth pangs of her unborn child, Jesus in his last moments of freedom recognises his role in birthing a new way of living.

The fourteenth-century English mystic, Mother Julian of Norwich, went to some lengths in describing the crucified Jesus as the mother in labour, forcing forth with cries of pain and acute suffering new life for all. She is not just using a literary allusion; she is speaking with the same language about Jesus as he used of himself. He can, indeed, be referred to as 'our true Mother Jesus'.

Jesus clearly demonstrates the major sexual movements I have outlined. He is concerned both with entering us, and inviting us to himself. In Revelation 3, verse 20, he is quoted as saying: 'Here I am! I stand at the door and knock. If anyone hears my voice and opens the door, I will come in. . .'

This text has been preached on throughout the history of the Christian church as Christ's plea to enter us, to fill us with his grace, to overwhelm us with his love. There is a very real sense in which the church has championed this very masculine Lord. And for good reason. As we have seen, Jesus is a masculine being.

And yet, time and time again, he is concerned that we enter into him. In the Gospels, he is often found saying that we must enter through the narrow gate and that he is the doorway, the entrance to God's presence. He is forever inviting us to enter through himself, to be enveloped by his grace. Both these movements echo the sexual movements of human and divine nature.

9

GOD AND GRACE

How we can be transformed by the Divine Lover

> *Do you know what it means to be struck by grace? . .*
> *We cannot transform our lives, unless we allow them to*
> *be transformed by that stroke of grace. It happens; or it*
> *does not happen.*
>
> Paul Tillich
>
> *The most beautiful and profound emotion we can*
> *experience is the sensation of the mystical.*
>
> Albert Einstein

WHAT HAVE WE SAID SO FAR? We have taken a look at the differences between masculinity and femininity and recognised that these differences belie fundamental differences not just in our sexual orientation, but in our spiritual inclinations as well. We have tracked these back to basic differences within the character of God and found that he reflects masculine and feminine 'movements'. This makes perfect sense, since he is the source of all human existence.

We have then suggested that, since God is the image of perfection, becoming more like God is a basic human desire. We become more like God when we learn to integrate both masculine and feminine character traits within each of us, since God is perfectly integrated in these ways. Then we took a look at Jesus as the human reflection of God to see what his sexuality looked like and picked up more clues regarding our own need to be more integrated.

If you can buy all this so far, it begs two core questions:

* How then can I respond to this God you have been talking about? *and*
* How then am I to respond to members of the opposite sex?

We will deal with each of these questions in this chapter and the next but, in short, the answer involves the transforming power of *grace!*

If my nature, which obviously includes my sexuality, reflects the nature of God in whom I find my true destiny, how do I respond to him? Surely not sexually!

Well, yes and no. Of course, our response to God is not sexual in the purely physical sense. To think so is silliness, though for centuries pagan religions have believed so. However, if by the term 'sexual' we mean the broader, all-encompassing definition which includes my spirituality, my values, my likes and dislikes, my attractions and repulsions, then yes, I can respond to God sexually. I can respond to God in my masculinity, as can my wife and daughters in their femininity.

This ought not to disturb us. The Jewish writers of centuries ago were quite prepared to think of our relationship with God in these terms. Comparing the interaction between God and humans with an affair between two lovers was quite acceptable. Some of their material has even found its way into the Old Testament.

✠ Hosea's picture of the Divine Lover

By far the most provocative and disturbing of this material is found in the book of Hosea. In this book, God is explicitly compared to a faithful lover whose partner has scorned him. The partner turns out to be symbolic of the people of Israel. Hosea cleverly uses explicitly sexual imagery to illustrate the passion and the compassion of God in the face of the unrelenting unfaithfulness of his people. And there's a very important reason for him using such language. In fact, if we're to understand the potency of this story, we need to do a little historical digging at its foundations.

During the time of Hosea — eight centuries before Christ — the Jewish nation had become enamoured of the pagan, sexual rites of various other neighbouring nations. Chief among them was the Canaanites. You can imagine it was difficult to maintain the strict practices of sexual fidelity required by Jewish law when everyone around you was engaging in all manner of exotic sexual behaviour as part of their religious systems.

Israel fell gradually into the trap of reflecting the practices of those around them. The Canaanites had developed a sexual rite that expected all young virgins to offer themselves for intercourse with strangers to bring new vitality to the clan. It appears that it happened only once in a woman's lifetime, so we should be careful not to confuse it with the other common practice of permanent prostitution supplied by the cult. While prostitutes serviced cult members regularly, the practice of offering young virgins was another — related — rite.

In Babylon, every native-born woman must once in her life enter the temple of Aphrodite and have intercourse with a stranger. In Phoenecia, men were expected to offer the gift of prostituting their daughters before the goddess Venus to receive her fullest blessing. And the Amorites developed the custom of having every bride sit at the temple door for seven days and engage in sexual intercourse with strangers before she could be married.

It might seem like little wonder that the Israelites were infected with such behaviour. The Canaanites' worship of Ba'al became a very acceptable feature of Jewish religion by the masses. In chapter 5, there is the story of Elijah's fiery encounter with the prophets of Ba'al which had occurred years before. So great were the inroads of Canaanite sexual rites that even Israel developed a pattern of religious practice that had young virgins 'initiated' into the cult, whereby the power of procreation was expected from Ba'al by 'having her womb opened in his sanctuary'.

A further, associated practice that arose out of this fertility cult was the sacrificing of one's firstborn child. This was based on the belief that, since the mother had acquired her ability to bear children in marriage by her participation in a pagan rite, she must give that child back to the divinity. Thereafter, legitimate marriage can begin and subsequent children can be kept.

It is difficult, historically, to determine how wide-spread this practice had become. There is evidence that orgiastic celebrations were also being practised by Jews in Israel. We should be aware that Israel was originally formed out of a union of Canaanite cities and tribal Jewish districts, so the impact of Canaan's cults on subsequent Jewish practice was bound to be difficult to unravel. It's enough to say that such practice was deemed to be barbaric licentiousness by Jewish law and those prophets, priests and political rulers who were committed to Israel's faith took severe measures against it (such as Elijah, for instance).

Let's just make this point again more clearly. Israel was surrounded by nations who related to their gods sexually. The chief expression of this relationship was through literal, physical sexual rites performed upon young virgins and indentured prostitutes primarily. Israel, smack-bang in the midst of all this action, caved in and, in spite of strong warnings to the contrary in their laws and teaching, embraced the sexual cult of Ba'al.

Now if this kind of behaviour is what is meant when I suggest that we can relate to God sexually, then I am to be condemned along with the misogynist fertility cult prophets. But this is not what I'm saying. I want to say just what Hosea himself said many centuries ago.

Hosea takes a very different line to Elijah. That prophet challenged the prophets of Ba'al to a showdown in a dramatic display of antagonism. There was no room for compromise or conciliation with Elijah. It was a win-lose situation that the Ba'al worshippers clearly lost. But Hosea's approach is altogether different. Hosea, rather than rejecting sexual rites and pagan cult worship outright, actually makes use of the language and mythology of those cults for his own ends. He doesn't deny that we can relate sexually to our God, but he does modify the way we might do so.

Hosea provided us with the astonishing idea of a legal marriage between God — who, in Israelite thought, was considered transsexual — and Israel herself. Before Hosea's time, this concept is absent in the Old Testament. It was his innovation. He is using pagan imagery to say something very important about how God relates to those he loves.

Hosea adopts this idea of a marriage between a god and his people from the very Canaanite mythology he is seeking to condemn and uses it in his polemic. Of course, the aspect of literal physical intercourse as symbolic of this relationship is excluded, but marriage imagery of intimacy, compassion, passion, desire, commitment, loyalty and so on are strongly suggested in Hosea's thinking. It was later picked up by other Old Testament writers like Jeremiah and Ezekiel, but here it occurs for the first time.

In fact, this tells us rather more than just about how we might relate to God holistically, including with our sexuality. It is a reminder to us that there is more than one way to confront those with whom we disagree theologically. Elijah is confrontational, competitive and aggressive in his disagreement with the Ba'al worshippers of Canaan. Hosea is inclusive, respectful and intuitive. Elijah taunts and scoffs his rivals. Hosea uses their very language and longings. Both are regarded as great Hebrew prophets, yet their approaches are completely different. So again we find hints of both masculine and feminine movements equally esteemed in the Bible.

In the first chapter of his book, Hosea says that God spoke to him and told him, 'Go, take to yourself an adulterous wife. . .' — referred to as a 'wife of whoredom' (verse 2). But this could simply be referring to any young woman ready for marriage who had submitted to the pagan sexual rites of initiation that were being performed at the time. She could be recognisable as an average, modern Israelite woman. So she whom Hosea is to marry is therefore not an especially wicked exception; she is simply representative of her contemporaries in Israel.

I'm not sure whether we can comprehend the potency of this command. Pure Israelite men were commanded to have nothing to do with sexual rites and certainly nothing to do with women who had been offered as sexual objects to pagan gods. Yet here was God telling his own prophet to sleep with a defiled woman.

It's not that Hosea's contemporaries weren't themselves engaging in this kind of practice. But for a 'holy man', God's spokesperson himself, to commit this sin would have been shocking. From the beginning of the story, Hosea's message is provocative and disturbing. In any case, the command to marry and sleep with a whore — an action that was considered atrocious — draws a picture of Israel's readiness for God's judgment.

Since the prophet is expected to take a 'wife of whoredom', it becomes startlingly clear to him and his people how complete Israel's corruption and guilt have become. Verse 2 continues: '. . .because the land is guilty of the vilest adultery in departing from the Lord'. A literal translation from Hebrew goes: '. . .the land is guilty of a-whoring away from the Lord'.

'A-whoring away from the Lord' — a graphic expression — calls to mind not just the sexual rites mentioned above, but a profusion of Canaanite fertility cults which had the 'land' under the mastery of the Mother Goddess. Not only were young virgins made fertile by Ba'al; the land was made fertile by the orgiastic pleasure and conception of the Mother Goddess as represented by her followers.

It all sounds pretty bizarre, doesn't it? Women were treated as objects of religious practice, no more highly regarded than talismans. Sex was perceived as having nothing to do with intimacy, trust or respect, but as a ritualistic activity guaranteeing rain, sunshine or human fertility. Into this depraved situation walks a young prophet, still committed to the old Jewish laws regarding fidelity, commitment and loyalty, who takes to his bed a victim of the barbarism around him.

Is he relinquishing his faith in these laws? Is he compromising his principles? Has he been seduced by Canaanite practices? None of the above. He is illustrating the extent of the depravity about him and the lengths to which God will go to bring his people back.

As I mentioned earlier, when discussing the motherly qualities of God, we have to be very cautious about not going back to the worship of a Mother Goddess when we consider all that's involved. In fact, it occasionally astounds me when I enter New Age bookshops to discover an increasing interest in Mother Goddess fertility cults. There would seem to be little to commend these cults when we realise that they ignore individual human dignity and treat women with contempt. They are, in their original form, violent and oppressive.

In Hosea's story, his adulterous wife, Gomer, having borne several children, leaves him, possibly for another man or maybe even to continue whoring. Hosea, compelled by his loyalty and devotion to her, resolves to take her back. He is forced to pay for her with silver and barley, indicating she has more than likely turned to prostitution. The unquestionable theme is of God's inability to stop loving his people in spite of their 'whoring' and unfaithfulness. Therefore, God's love becomes a model for Hosea's love; it stands in contrast to the fickle lovers for whom God's love remains true. Its overpowering strength suddenly becomes apparent as it is reflected in the prophet's symbolic action.

Not only was God's original command to marry an adulteress jarring to Hosea's original readers; this second command — to buy her back out of her unfaithfulness — would have been just as disturbing. In Jewish law as stated in Deuteronomy 24, verses 1 to 4, even a lawfully divorced and remarried woman must not return to her first husband. Now, however, the love of Hosea, which represents the love of God, is to bring home an adulteress who had legally come into another's possession! God does what is impossible according to the law. His love overrules his justice.

The power of this story, and in particular the very brief third chapter in which this reconciliation occurs, can barely be fully understood today. It shames the people of Israel. Rather than calling down the fire of judgment from heaven, Hosea opens heaven's gate to allow the people a rare glimpse of the heartbroken and humiliated God who has loved them despite their unfaithfulness.

This idea was pursued by the apostle Paul in his letter to the Romans (chapter 8, verse 3): 'For what the law was powerless to do in that it was weakened by the sinful nature, God did by sending his own Son in the likeness of sinful man to be a sin offering. . .' In other words, the law of judgment becomes impotent in the face of rampant, unchecked debauchery as was the case in Israel during Hosea's time and in the Roman Empire during Paul's. When people choose to ignore the law, only love will do the trick. For Hosea, that expression of love was in the form of fifteen shekels of silver and a handful of barley, the price he paid for his wayward wife. For Paul, God's love was expressed in the sacrifice of his Son for the sins of the wayward world.

How do we respond to such a God? We had better be prepared to acknowledge that this God is so devoted to his people that his passion cannot be extinguished. He adores us as Hosea adored Gomer. Is there a sexual component to this imagery? Absolutely! God does not demand sexual rites of his people — in fact, he bans them — but he does allow sexually-charged imagery to be used to illustrate his loyalty toward and desire for his people.

At many of the weddings I have conducted as a minister of religion, I have drawn attention to this biblical allusion. As the bride first appears at the door of the church and begins to proceed down the aisle, I am not so much looking at her, but at her husband-to-be. At his first glimpse of her, the groom will often gasp ever so slightly or grin foolishly at the sight of his gorgeous bride. It's not uncommon for me, when conducting the ceremony, to point out this small, often unnoticed detail to the assembled guests.

'Did you notice his breath being snapped off?' I will ask them, 'Did you see his wide, involuntary grin? Did you notice the sheer adoration and desire with which he observed this woman coming towards him? Well, if you did, remember this; the love and desire this man feels for this woman at this moment is only an inkling of the love God feels for you.'

This is the message of Hosea. So powerful was this illustration of human sexual love as a symbol of divine love that it was picked up later by other Jewish thinkers and writers. The prophet Jeremiah simply reiterates Hosea's ideas when he says in Jeremiah 3, verse 1:

> *If a man divorces his wife and*
> *she leaves him and marries another man,*
> *should he return to her again?*
> *Would not the land be completely defiled?*
> *But you have lived as a prostitute*
> *with many lovers ----*
> *would you now return to me?'*
> *declares the Lord.*

How touching, that after declaring how impossible it is for an adulterous wife to return to her first husband, God should still yearn for such an unlikely reconciliation with his people. 'Would you now return to me?' is a truly poignant plea from him. How would the people respond? Jeremiah in verses 22 and 23 writes out a response typical of the one God yearns to hear:

'Yes, we will come to you,
  for you are the Lord our God.
Surely the idolatrous commotion on
  the hills and mountains is a deception;
surely in the LORD our God
  is the salvation of Israel. . .'

The idolatrous commotion mentioned is a reference to the pagan fertility practices that invariably occurred on high places like hills or mountains. Jeremiah, so desperate to see his people turn back to their God, puts words of repentance in their mouths to little avail.

Insofar as we can tell, Jeremiah's message fell on deaf ears. The idolatrous commotion went on well into the dark night of Israel's history while God burned with his passion for an unfaithful people.

✠ Ezekiel's picture of the Divine Lover

There is no question that the most explicit retelling of Hosea's notion of God as a faithful husband and his people as a promiscuous bride occurs in the very frank sixteenth chapter of Ezekiel. Just in case you thought Bible stories were just for children in Sunday schools, think again.

Ezekiel takes Hosea's already provocative imagery and presses it even further. If you ever doubted the sexual component to our relationship with God, this chapter will be certain to force a re-evaluation. A warning to the squeamish: this could be quite disturbing.

Ezekiel 16 begins in the usual way: 'The word of the Lord came to me: "Son of man, confront Jerusalem with her detestable practices and say, 'This is what the

Sovereign Lord says to Jerusalem. . .'"' But Ezekiel, not one noted for his subtlety, then takes confrontation to new heights. He personifies Israel as a newly-birthed child of foreign parents in verses 4 and 5:

> *On the day you were born your cord was not cut, nor were you washed with water to make you clean, nor were you rubbed with salt or wrapped in cloths.*
> *No-one looked on you with pity or had compassion enough to do any of these things for you. Rather, you were thrown out into the open field, for on the day you were born you were despised.*

As if this image of an abandoned and uncleaned new-born infant isn't gruesome enough, Ezekiel spells it out even further by having God say:

> *Then I passed by and saw you kicking about in your blood, and as you lay there in your blood I said to you 'Live!'*

He is daring to suggest that Israel, of questionable parentage, is like an abandoned child lying in an open field covered in blood and birth fluid and afterbirth, her umbilical cord still unsevered. The picture is a powerful, even offensive reminder of Israel's inauspicious beginnings. Even today, the Palestinian custom is to rub a newly-born infant with salt, water and oil and to bind it tightly for seven days in bands, after which a further washing and rubbing takes place.

God is saying through Ezekiel that the newly-born nation of Israel had nothing to commend it. No-one loved her enough to perform these elementary duties.

Israel wasn't born of fine pedigree. Neither was she ever destined for great things. She was even despised by the nations that 'formed' her, the Canaanites and Amorites and Hittites. In effect, God is saying: 'From the moment you were born — the moment you arrived in Canaan — you have been abandoned. From the day you were born naked in this world, you have been unwanted.'

Nevertheless, as gory as this bizarre image might be, Ezekiel is actually going to tell a love story. God, like a young king travelling in the fields, happens upon the abandoned girl-child and encourages her to live. When no-one else will, God offers her a chance at life. His patronage over the years, however, is to blossom into so much more than charity as verse 7 makes clear: 'I made you grow like a plant of the field. You grew up and developed and became the most beautiful of jewels. Your breasts were formed and your hair grew, you who were naked and bare.'

This is sexually charged language. As God, like a guardian, cares for the unwanted baby, he watches her grow. He notices her body becoming shapely and womanly and her hair growing thick and luxuriant. This is not just her guardian talking. This is a man with desire in his eyes. Soon, as verse 8 shows, that desire turns to lovemaking:

> Later I passed by, and when I looked at you and saw that you were old enough for love, I spread the corner of my garment over you and covered your nakedness. I gave you my solemn oath and entered into a covenant with you, declares the Sovereign Lord, and you became mine.

After this he bathes her, dresses her lavishly and adorns her with fine jewellery. Her beauty, already remarkable but disguised by her common beginnings, is now clear to all. The beautiful and radiant queen is famous throughout the land. Every nation seems to love the story of a commoner marrying a king. Well, here we have a classic rags-to-riches love story. But it is a love story about to turn very sour.

'But you trusted in your beauty and used your fame to become a prostitute.' So begins the fifteenth verse of this chapter which marks the turning point of the illustration. Already an erotic tale of desire and passion, love and redemption, the story degenerates into a litany of despicable and wretched sexual practices engaged in by the young queen.

She uses her beautiful garments in erotic behaviour on the high places where the fertility cults carried on their orgies. She melts down her jewellery and fashions them into sexual devices to be used in ritualistic masturbation. She offers her possessions as sacrifices to the idols. She even presents her children as living sacrifices to the fertility gods. Every good gift her lover has bestowed upon her is corrupted and used in the evil and barbaric rituals of the pagan gods. The shame of her husband, the humiliation, is palpable.

There is such an undercurrent of violence running through Ezekiel that it's very difficult to read sometimes. By 'violence', I mean an unspoken sense that at any minute, something even more dreadful than what has just taken place is about to occur. As we imagine (if we dare to imagine) the disgraceful behaviour of the commoner-queen on the hills of Palestine, we can't bare to think of what the king will do to her. I guess we project ourselves into the story and feel the jealousy and rage, the humiliation and shame that the king might have felt.

The Australian-New Zealand film, *The Piano*, does this very well, too. The character of Ada's husband played by Sam Neil virtually seethes with frustration and jealousy for much of the film. We are waiting breathlessly to see how he will react to his wife's increasing infidelity. When finally he does explode, severing one of her fingers with an axe, our greatest fears are confirmed. In fact, when he captures her and drags her to the chopping block, his axe in hand, we fear he might do worse than mutilate her hand.

Well, in Ezekiel's sordid tale of promiscuity and debauchery, God, like Sam Neil's character, can bare it no longer and wails with pain and grief. From verse 23 to nearly the end of the chapter, he recalls her dreadful exploits. He rehearses the names of her lovers and recounts how insatiable her sexual appetite has become. As difficult as it might have been, he recalls the details of her prostitution.

I've heard from marriage counsellors that this is a common response to the infidelity of a marriage partner. Within the innocent partner, there is an almost pathological desire to know every last detail of the affair, even though they realise that knowing such details will hurt them even more. In his pain and humiliation, God calls her names and dreams of ways he might punish her. It is a graphic and pathetic display by one whose love knows no bounds and whose shame knows no greater depths.

Nevertheless, just as it appeared in Hosea's story and in Jeremiah's use of this imagery, God's love and grace and forgiveness always wins the day. The final verses — verses 60 and 63 — of the chapter rise slowly (and almost begrudgingly) from the morass of anger and condemnation:

'Yet I will remember the covenant I made with you in the days of your youth, and I will establish an everlasting covenant with you. . . Then, when I make atonement for you for all you have done, you will remember and be ashamed and never again open your mouth because of your humiliation,' declares the Sovereign Lord.

✠ Modern reflections on ancient stories of the Divine Lover

How are we to respond to God? Like one who has scorned a lover's advances and realised we've missed a good thing? This is very basic Judeo-Christian theology. We have turned away from God's loving embrace, but he still welcomes us back in spite of where we've been. It's called grace. My point is that the Old Testament writers were not shy about couching the concept of grace in very sexual or romantic terms. God loves us. He wants to woo and win us. We have, for the most part, behaved as Israel behaved — contemptibly.

Nonetheless, God's powerful, loving embrace is still open to us. Surely, this has a sexual component! Not that it involves ritualistic sexual intercourse to express it. This is the very behaviour Hosea and the others were condemning. But does God desire us? You bet. He has watched us grow from ugly ducklings as our breasts formed and our hair grew. He has spied us from afar as we have become old enough for love. He wants to take us under the corner of his garment and make us his.

In 1924, the poet and novelist, Charles Williams, ventured a rare attempt (for him) at theological writing with his booklet, *Outlines of Romantic Theology*. Williams was a well-known member of the Inklings, the group of creative Oxford Christians of the 1930s and 1940s that included C.S. Lewis and J.R.R. Tolkien. In it, he explains his theory — already implicit in his poetry — that human romantic love can enhance our apprehension of God.

Williams points out that theology has traditionally used common phenomena to help unfold our understanding of God — for example, experiences of nature in natural theology, ethical choices in moral theology and human reasoning in dogmatic theology. But the one experience most common and universal to humans — the romantic love of two people — is rarely or adequately used as a way of gaining insight into God's nature.

For Charles Williams, in experiencing romantic love we experience God. God has been in the experience from the beginning and the more we learn about it, the more we learn also about him. Remember, that romantic love is different from the kind of robust love we talked about in chapter 5. Romantic love is based on feelings and affections. Real loving is based on loyalty, hard work and courage. Nevertheless, this is not to say the intoxicating feeling of 'falling in love' can't give us important clues to the way we relate to God and he to us. The erotic and overwhelming sensations of desire, passion, jealousy and arousal are all apparent in Hosea, Jeremiah and Ezekiel.

It's time to be less prudish about the language we use and the sensations we embrace in our thinking about God. He seems perfectly prepared to access us intellectually, emotionally, morally or sexually. How are we to respond to him?

In essence, what I am saying is that the very gospel itself is 'sexy' in its intent. It is about a devoted God who is remarkably attracted to us and won't take 'no' for an answer. His passion, his desire to make us his own, knows no bounds. But we, like Israel, like Hosea's wife, have gone off a-whoring. We have all abandoned our highest and best ideals. We have not loved or cared enough. We have not pursued justice or mercy enough. We are selfish, frightened and lazy.

My two most apparent qualities are fear and laziness. Okay, it's true I haven't headed off to the hills to engage in ritualised orgies. It's true I pay my taxes, cut my lawns, wash my car and send my kids off to good schools. But I can't get away from the fact that my fear and my laziness limit my potential for wholeness. I make offerings to these gods every day, knowing that the God who loves me like a king wants to take me, ravish me, cover my nakedness and help me fulfil my potential.

Just as Hosea pays for his wife in silver and barley and Ezekiel's king pays for his with atoning sacrifices, God pays for me. Not with money, for there isn't enough money in the world to pay for me. He pays with blood, with the life of his Son, Jesus.

The realisation that my God has done this for me can't help but invade every aspect of my psyche, including my sexuality. It's called grace. And encounters with grace are transforming experiences. We need to be prepared to allow God to ravish us with his steadfast and loyal love.

✠ A personal encounter with the Divine Lover

It seems to me that it's entirely appropriate to compare significant religious experiences with a feeling of having been completely ravished. My first truly significant experience of being overwhelmed by God's seductive power was in August 1991 when I attended a conference in Darling Harbour in Sydney at which the key speaker was the American writer and psychiatrist, M. Scott Peck.

Peck is a bit of a hero of mine. He's probably best known as the author of *The Road Less Travelled*, as well as other titles such as *The Different Drum, People of the Lie,* and *A World Waiting to be Born.* He has a knack of being able to fuse good psychological insights, traditional values and simple Christian theology in a way that offers good commonsense approaches to achieving spiritual wholeness. And since I have a personal conviction to bring Christian theology to bear on the issues of modern living in ways that make sense of both real life and biblical theology, I'm very impressed with his efforts.

What are you like when you encounter an author who says on paper what you already think in your mind and know in your body to be true about life, relationships and the journey toward wholeness? There are times when a writer will seem to put into words things you already believed to be true, but had never articulated in formal words or thoughts. Those books or authors become part of the precious lexicon that makes up the body of our own unique philosophies and ways of being and knowing.

I have a whole swag of books, quotes, poems, songs, articles and chapters photocopied out of various books that have proved important in my spiritual pilgrimage. I find it's hard not to form something of an attachment to those authors who have offered me something in the way of helping me to formulate my own words for saying what I think about life. As a result, I've always felt close to a number of people I've never actually met and in some cases certainly never will.

One of those is Scott Peck so, when it was announced that he was touring Australia in 1991, I felt it was my chance to meet one of my literary mentors. I eagerly registered for the conference. To my amazement, this ended up not being a chance to meet Scott Peck, but to encounter God in the most alarming, sexual kind of way.

Peck's final lecture of the conference was called 'Sexuality and Spirituality'. I pricked my ears up in anticipation. His material was delightful and stimulating. But it was his finale that was to blow my socks off. After speaking about the way God can access us sexually and spiritually, he announced that he wanted to conclude the seminar with an interactive illustration of his point.

He told us he was going to play a song over the sound system. It was a Cat Stevens song, an old 'sixties love song, overlaid with the full, lusty acoustic guitar sound so much a feature of his music. The song is called 'Can't Keep It In'. Whether you know it will depend on whether you're a baby boomer or not. Peck asked us to listen to the music and to follow along with the lyrics on the song sheet provided in our conference notes. And, as we do this, he said, we are to imagine our lovers singing this song to us. 'Picture your wives, husbands, lovers, boyfriends, girlfriends, and imagine that they are saying these words to you as they're being played over the sound system,' he said.

I tried to enter into the exercise as best I could, but I suspected from the outset that I wasn't going to manage it very effectively. Typical of many Cat Stevens' songs, it has a strong, masculine, demanding lyric, which invites the listener to be 'taken', conquered and ravished. I don't doubt Carolyn's deep love for me, but as much as I tried to hear her expressing such a powerful, masculine urge to 'have' me, it was no use.

Frustrated with myself, I listened to the song and read along with the words:

Oh, I can't keep it in, can't keep it in,
I've gotta let it out,
I've gotta show all the world, world's gotta see,
See all the love, love that's in me ---- I said
Why walk alone? Why worry when it's warm over here?
You've got so much to say, say what you mean,
Mean what you think, and think anything.
Oh why, why must you waste your life away?

You've got to live for today, then let it go ---- oh,
Lover, I want to spend this time with you,
There's nothing I wouldn't do, if you let me know ----
And I can't keep it in, I can't hide it and
I can't lock it away.
I'm up for your love, love heats my blood,
Blood spins my head, and my head falls in love.
No, I can't keep it in, I can't keep it in,
I've gotta let it out.
I've gotta show all the world, world's gotta know,
Know of the love, love that lies low, so
Why can't you say, if you know then
Why can't you say?
You've got too much deceit, and deceit kills the light.
Light needs to shine. I said shine light, shine light. . .[1]

There's more, but you get the idea? Well, during
the playing of this song, something surprising and overwhelming began to occur to me. I say 'occur to me',
but I'm not actually aware of it ever really 'occurring'
to me at all. In fact, it seemed hardly a cognitive
response at all. I didn't think about what I was experiencing. I just felt it. And I felt it very powerfully. It
dawned on me in this wonderfully non-cognitive way
that this wasn't my wife singing this demanding song of
masculine love. It could be *God*! And since I had never
experienced God in this powerfully sensual way before,
it scared the daylights out of me and thrilled me at the
very same time.

I felt drawn into the wildly sensual and erotic feeling
of being seduced by God. I knew this not just with my
mind, but in my body, with my spirit, in my being: that
God desired me, wanted me and was demanding that I

be his. I had never so powerfully experienced God as being so masculine as I did that day. All my life I had heard God being referred to by the masculine pronoun. All my life I had heard about God as 'he' or 'him', but had never before sensed his powerful masculinity before.

I knew he was demanding that I be his, that he have me, ravish me, that he seduce me. The language is strongly sexual, but I don't recall this being an explicitly sexual experience for me. All I recall is that in the very depths of my soul I sensed God's unrelenting love and acceptance and that this invaded my sexuality, my spirituality, my intellectual and emotional being, my everything, my all.

In many respects, I felt the kind of devotion and grace that Hosea and Ezekiel and Jeremiah detail in their writings. I felt like Hosea's wife, Gomer, or the whoring queen in Ezekiel 16 when confronted with my Lover's remarkable love.

Now a Cat Stevens song only lasts three to four minutes tops, so this was not exactly a lingering experience. Yet strangely, as delicious as this sensation was, I was relieved it was so brief. I was feeling decidedly uncomfortable about it all and resolved to reflect on it later. But obviously Scott Peck was on my wavelength (or I was on his) because, after the music had finished, he announced that he was about to play the song again. 'Only this time,' he said, 'I want you to imagine that *God is singing this song to you!*'

Well, that was all the prompting I needed. As the song played through the second time, I wept like there was no tomorrow. It was one of the most remarkably healing experiences of my life. I was overwhelmed by God's grace, by his sheer, unadulterated love for me. Can you imagine God saying, 'Oh, I can't keep it in. I've gotta let it out. I've gotta show all the world. The world's gotta see all the love that's in me.' To imagine hearing God speak in this enthusiastic manner and see him as just not being able to wait to make me his was a peculiar experience and one that transformed my way of understanding him and myself.

When I heard him say, 'You've got too much deceit. And deceit kills the light. Light needs to shine', I sobbed uncontrollably. There were no words to express my gratitude, my humility. I can now reflect on the words of Ezekiel 16, verse 63: 'Then, when I make atonement for you for all you have done, you will remember and be ashamed and never again open your mouth because of your humiliation. . .' This was how I felt, like the commoner queen-turned-whore.

My humiliation at having presumed I understood God in my mind or in my ritualised religious practices was palpable. Here was God demanding I bow before him in the totality of my being — that I was to understand him within my spirit, my sexuality, my whole psyche and my body. An encounter with grace is both the most debilitating and exhilarating of all experiences. It is one that I will treasure forever.

It occurred to me that this was an entirely religious Christian experience. But what had disturbed me was that I wasn't sensing it as you might expect a 'normal' Christian experience to feel. Here I was feeling *ravished* by God. I felt like I'd just been seduced by the creator of heaven and earth! This dual experience of spirituality and sexuality is not one usually encouraged by the Christian church — but how could I deny my experience?

The awesome power of being overwhelmed by God's gracious desire forced me to make radical re-evaluations about my view of God and the way God interacts with human beings. Perhaps God, I thought, actually prefers to encounter us in the whole of our humanness, rather than just in the cognitive or moral/ethical or spiritual elements of our nature. Maybe God demands to woo us and win us and to encounter us as much through our sexuality as through any other avenue of human experience.

✠ Israel's King David and the Divine Lover

There is a delightful little story in the Old Testament concerning a man who I'm sure felt as overwhelmed by God's pleasure as I did that day at Darling Harbour. His name is King David. In 2 Samuel 6, there is the story about the day the ark of the covenant was finally brought to David's capital, Jerusalem.

We need to remember that for the Hebrews, God's very presence resided in this mystical box. You might have seen Steven Spielberg's *Raiders of the Lost Ark* — a fanciful and superstitious depiction of the ark. But in some respects, the Hebrews treated the ark with the kind of respect and reverence shown by Indiana Jones. They believed the Law of Moses, the tangible evidence of God's covenant with Israel, was contained in the ornate chest. Therefore, wherever the ark was, there was God.

Later in their history, they realised that God was beyond being contained in boxes, tabernacle or temples, but these were early days and their thinking was less sophisticated than later.

So you can imagine how delighted the king of Israel, having recently routed the Philistines, would have been to be able finally to negotiate the removal of the ark from Judah to his own city, the capital, Jerusalem. It was said that whoever treated the ark with irreverence would be struck dead, but whoever protected the box and respected it would be greatly blessed.

Ever so carefully, with respect that bordered on fear, David moved the ark from Judah to Jerusalem. It would have seemed that everything was complete. Israel had been victorious and was now prospering, her enemies were defeated, her capital was secure and, now, the presence of God was safe within the walls of Jerusalem.

If ever there was an experience of God's overwhelming grace, this was it. God had blessed David and his nation beyond expectations and they believed they owed it all to him. As the ark was being ceremonially brought into the city, David, so rapt in sheer delight and spiritual ecstasy, does the most astounding thing: he tears off his clothes and dances and gambols and frolics virtually nude in the presence of God. Sounds bizarre, doesn't it?

Well, he's not quite nude. He wears a single garment, an ephod — a close-fitting sleeveless vest worn by the high priest under his breastpiece, girdle and robe. In effect, it was an ornate piece of underwear, made from choice, expensive materials, including thin gold wire threads, purple, blue and scarlet cloth, and finely woven linen. The ephod was fastened at the shoulder by clasps, to which were attached two onyx stones engraved with the names of the twelve tribes of Israel. It reached to about the waist. Over it was placed a waistband or girdle and dazzling breastpiece decorated with precious stones. The traditional royal blue robe was fastened around the hips and fell to floor length. There was no question that the high priest in his full regalia was quite a sight.

As the ark was brought into the capital, the residents of Jerusalem lined the roadways and trumpets blared and all the pomp and ceremony that the small nation could muster was laid on. And David, the conquering king, like a dancing jester or court clown, disrobes and pulls on the high priest's sacred undergarment and dances through the streets with all his might. So overwhelmed was he by God's grace that David, like an innocent child, dances semi-naked without shame or any sense of self-consciousness whatsoever. It is a charming display of utter joy and ecstasy.

Michal, the daughter of David's predecessor, King Saul, watching from her palace window, is disgusted by what she believes is a sordid and undignified display. In many respects encounters with grace *are* pretty undignified displays. The day I cried like a baby before God's grace, I didn't feel too dignified at all.

Verse 20 of 2 Samuel 6 records how Michal storms into David's court later in the day and bellows: 'How the king of Israel has distinguished himself today, disrobing in the sight of the slave girls of his servants as any vulgar fellow would!' And David's response in verses 21 and 22 is as sweet as it comes:

> *It was before the Lord, who chose me rather than your father or anyone from his house when he appointed me ruler over the Lord's people Israel ---- I will celebrate before the Lord. I will become even more undignified than this, and I will be humiliated in my own eyes. But by these slave girls you spoke of, I will be held in honour.*

An encounter with God's grace is like that; it makes you feel humiliated and honoured at the same time, like the whoring queen in Ezekiel and the dancing King David equally and at the same time.

Do you remember all our talk of paradox earlier? This is the usual response to a meaningful encounter with the paradoxical God who is both holy and loving, both judging and gracious. We can only respond paradoxically; we can only be aware of both our abject humility and shame *and* our sheer joy and blessed relief.

In a sense, you feel both miniscule and unimportant in the scheme of things *and* full of pride and worth. When you meet this living God, your mouth will be closed in his presence because you sense your lack of worth before him, but you'll also feel like gambolling nude like a child who feels no shame and knows that the world is a friendly place.

In many respects, this is the potency of God's seductive love. Of course it's sexual. Not that God has sex with us or any other such silliness. Rather, he encounters us at such a great depth of human experience that it *must* include our sexuality.

✠ Jesus' parable of an encounter with the Divine Lover

Jesus was perfectly comfortable with speaking of himself and God in sexually charged ways. In Matthew 25, he refers to himself as a bridegroom coming to take his bride to his bed. It's an intriguing parable. It concerns ten virgins awaiting their bridegroom one day.

We need to understand the marriage customs of Jesus' day to get the importance of the illustration. Normally, marriage involved three distinct stages. First, there was the engagement when the fathers of the prospective bride and groom met to hammer out the terms of the arrangement.

Second, there was the betrothal, which was a legally binding ceremony wherein the young man and the young woman contracted to be wed twelve months hence. This was not at all like the 'engagements' we see today, where young couples get engaged and un-engaged. Once betrothed, the couple were as good as married. Of course, the union wasn't consummated until the marriage ceremony proper.

Twelve months later, the third step would be completed when the groom would leave his home and proceed on foot down to his betrothed's home. She would have prepared herself for his coming and would be anticipating his arrival. Then, together and with their guests, they all proceed to the marriage ceremony and the community celebration that was to follow.

In this story, we have not one, but *ten* young virgins awaiting the groom. Scholars of biblical material have often scratched their heads about this one. Are the ten virgins bridesmaids or friends of the bride? Well, since the whole story has farcical elements to it, I think Jesus is being very cheeky, actually. He purposely does not make clear why there are ten brides in the story. Rather, he just goes on with the story.

Imagine, he suggests, that five of these virgins are wise and the other five are foolish. (Once when I was preaching on this passage and all those blonde jokes were doing the rounds, someone rudely asked from the congregation what hair colouring the foolish virgins had!) The wise virgins fill their lamps with oil, but the foolish virgins do not take oil. It is this preparation that distinguishes the wise from the foolish virgins, as we shall see.

As the ten of them wait for their lover to arrive, the clock ticks by. He doesn't come in the morning or at midday. He doesn't come in the afternoon or at dusk. He doesn't even come in the early evening. This in itself is part of the farce associated with Jesus' story. The unpredictable groom doesn't arrive to take his bride to his bed until midnight, the darkest hour of the evening. Then, the wise virgins light their full lamps trimmed with oil and dance out into the evening to meet their betrothed in the darkness.

But the foolish virgins cry out, 'How can we meet our lover? We have no oil in our lamps!' They beg the wise virgins to share their oil so they, too, can see their way, but the wise virgins refuse, telling them to go wake the oil salesman and buy their own oil for their lamps! At midnight, mind you! Then, in Jesus' tale, the wise virgins are taken into the wedding banquet to enjoy their lover forever and the foolish virgins, by the time they buy their oil and find their way to the feast, are refused admittance.

It's a farcical tale, not meant to be taken seriously for its absurd details. But its meaning is a very serious one. First, if we see Jesus as the bridegroom, the story implies that he can have many lovers — that his love and grace are available to as many who will come with him. Like giggling, excited brides, we are invited to be his lovers, to be taken by him to romp in the celestial hay forever. But the other meaning, the more confronting meaning, concerns the metaphor of the oil.

It wasn't until I studied biblical imagery that I realised that oil is a well-known symbol of preparation. Kings and priests were prepared for their roles by the anointing of oil. The wise virgins weren't being selfish and uncaring when they refused to share their oil. The point of the story is that we cannot do someone else's preparation for them. When Jesus the bridegroom comes to take us to be his, we cannot be prepared by someone else. We must do our own preparation. We must embrace God's grace for ourselves.

I have known a great many families where the parents have had a genuine and abiding faith in God and regular encounters with his grace. They have raised their children to be open to this same faith, but in some cases their children, when they have become adults, have abandoned their religion. In some cases they have virtually said something akin to, 'You can stick your religion wherever it fits, because I don't want to have anything to do with it ever again.' Understandably, this has caused their parents much grief. Some of these parents have told me that they wished they could do the preparation for their children, that they could fill their adult children's lamps with the oil of readiness for grace.

But the bottom line is this: we are all responsible for our own choices. Should we choose to ignore or run from experiencing God's grace, we will reap the repercussions for ourselves. Mummy and Daddy can no longer fill our lamps for us. When love comes to town, whether it be midnight or dawn, if we have not readied ourselves for such an encounter, it will pass us by.

This is another remarkable facet of grace. It always esteems the individual and refuses to force itself on the unwilling. But we should bear this in mind: being willing to encounter grace means being willing for humiliation; for an encounter with our own unworthiness. It's not pleasant being reminded that you've gone a-whoring in God's sight. But we've all done it to a greater or lesser degree. As feminist writer, Germaine Greer says, 'You are only liberated when you realise how awful you are.'

The charming, seductive, overwhelming grace and love of God will tantalise you and woo you. But God wants to love us, not use us. He respects the diffident and never acts against our will.

How can we respond to such a God? Like both a speechless, shameful whore and a dancing, frolicking king? It's always a paradox, isn't it?

10

ACCEPTING AND EXPRESSING GRACE

How we can show true love

The illumined walk without fear ---- by grace.
                                          Joel S. Goldsmith

*Some day after we have mastered the winds, the tides
and gravity, we will harness for God the energies of love;
and then, for the second time in the history of the world,
man will have discovered fire!*

                                          Pierre Teilhard de Chardin

HOW, THEN, ARE WE TO RESPOND TO EACH OTHER?
Simple! The way God responds to us: *by grace!*

The whole argument of this book has been heading
in this direction, hasn't it? If we find our source in God,
if we reflect the 'movements' of God with our gender
and if the path to human wholeness involves the integration of those two basic movements within every
individual, then the ultimate goal of humankind is to
become more like God. In other words, we are to
become more holy and more loving — and to express
this through our gender.

This will involve men becoming more loving and women more assertive — and everything that's involved with such a process of integration.

This has been termed, for men, as 'finding their feminine side'. I saw a television program recently that dealt with the way tough, rough, burly firemen were being taught to connect with their femininity in order to cope with the toll of human tragedy they often face in their job. Conversely, women are being trained in how to 'toughen up' and become more assertive, more apparently masculine.

This may be very well and good, but I think it misses the ultimate point. Men are not intended to be women, nor women men. Certainly, we need to integrate so-called opposite sex traits within our psyche. I'm very supportive of this. But when we do so, we should be assured that what we're actually doing is symptomatic of our yearning to be whole. When we abandon antiquated social expectations of femininity or masculinity, we are wising up and saying we want to be complete, to be perfect. We are yearning for spiritual/sexual wholeness. That is, we want to be like the one who created us — the only perfect one, God!

Isn't this the way we began this argument — by recognising C.S. Lewis' contention that all human yearning is the yearning for God? To be truly whole involves embracing the paradox of being both holy and loving, as God is. This will be reflected in our preparedness to tease out opposite sex traits that enable us to become more the one or the other. For example, men may need to work on being more prepared for intimacy, more likely to be moved by compassion or mercy, more loyal, more nurturing.

In doing so, we oughtn't to think this will make men more like women. We should think it will make them more like *God*! I cannot emphasise this point enough.

When my wife and I encourage our daughters to be more assertive, are we wanting them to grow up to be men? God is a jealous God, remember? By this we mean he displays tough love. He draws lines for his people and won't allow himself to be abused forever. This is clearly illustrated by Hosea and Ezekiel in the previous chapter. So, if we support our daughters in becoming more 'jealous', less of a pushover in relationships, less 'nurturing', perhaps tougher or more resilient, are we wanting them to be more masculine *or* more God-like?

One of my fundamental convictions in writing this book is that we have become far too concerned with *competitive* gender relations, whereby everyone is trying to be more like the other than the other ever was. I genuinely believe much of the confusion would dissipate if we could be prepared to be more like God and his child Jesus, the template of human perfection. That is, we need to embrace the paradoxes of being holy and being loving, of achievement and attachment, of penetration and invitation, of doing things and being things.

When we learn this difficult lesson, we are fit for greater humanness. Then, we are fit to recognise both our own unworthiness and the remarkable worth with which God sees us (another paradox). In other words, when we see that being God-like is our goal, we are better prepared to encounter him for ourselves.

Most of us are afraid of God, if the truth be known, because he is the perfect reminder of how far short we fall — and we don't enjoy being reminded of our inadequacy. But when we draw near to him, we encounter the miracle of God's grace, his mercy, his forgiveness, his tough love and his majesty. God's grace is offered to us in Christ and it makes all the difference. It draws back the veil between God and ourselves. It allows intimacy between God and ourselves. It makes God's nature all the clearer to us, which in turn makes us much clearer to ourselves. We can only be more whole, more like God, if we have a clear idea of what God looks like himself.

If grace is the key to intimacy between God and ourselves, then it stands to reason that grace is likewise the key to intimacy between human beings. When we embrace God's grace and become more God-like, we are far better resourced to become agents of grace in this world ourselves. And I believe this will transform human, including gender, relationships.

✠ Powerful cultural forces that downgrade human growth and value

But powerful forces have arisen to combat such peace and such growth towards wholeness. If there was any possibility that we, as humans, might look to the spiritual/ sexual clues built into our psyches and discover their source is in God, much of contemporary culture is mitigating against it.

Currently, Western popular culture is suggesting to us that femininity and masculinity has more to do with height, weight and breast size than it has with holiness, love or grace. On the one hand, I am saying that femininity, naturally concerned with attachment and invitation, needs to learn from God how to be more assertive, more effective while, on the other hand, scores of magazines are telling us that femininity is about weight loss, fashion sense, cosmetics and perfume. Something has gone awry.

We mustn't allow the media to fool us on this point. Our sexuality is a deep spiritual aspect to our nature. It is part of God's richness reflected in us. When we boil masculinity down to broad shoulders, prominent pectorals, corrugated stomach muscles and a full head of hair, we are falling back into the kind of inadequate genitality definitions we began with. And such inadequate definitions are all around us.

A little while ago, the ABC began broadcasting old episodes of the original *I Love Lucy* series. Since I could recall deriving a lot of pleasure from reruns of the shenanigans of Lucy and Ricky and Fred and Ethel, I was happy for my kids to watch it. That was until I began to watch it again myself.

Let's face it, the basic premise that undergirded every episode and from which most of the humour arose was the one that wives should be afraid of their husbands and should keep information from them. Most of Lucy's adventures revolved around her trying to hide something from Ricky, lest he be angry with her. In fact, at the close of one episode, he takes her across his knee and spanks her for misbehaving. This was not something we were eager for our daughters to view.

But in another disturbing episode, Lucy decides she wants to get a job and raises this with Ricky who, as in just about every other episode, is furious. He won't have any wife of his getting a job, thankyou very much. Ricky explains that Lucy's role is to care for the apartment (one room with a lounge in the middle), to prepare lovely meals for him and to look beautiful when he returns home each evening. Are you feeling ill yet?

Anyway, true to form, Lucy disregards Ricky's advice and goes looking for a part-time job she can keep from him. All manner of ridiculous scenarios ensue, until finally Lucy comes to her senses and admits to Ricky that she doesn't need a job, after all. It's enough for her to simply be 'Mrs Ricky Ricardo' — and she's proud of it. The audience applauds heartily and the credits roll.

Carolyn and I felt we needed to de-program our daughters after watching this nonsense. We explained to them that this show was about forty years old and that men and women don't relate to each other like this any more. I can recall explaining that a woman's role is not just to look beautiful for her man. There is more to femininity than this.

A few days later, I came home to discover my daughters glued to the screen watching *Baywatch*. Are you aware of the roles women play in the program? You guessed it. They're in the show to look beautiful and glamorous for their men. It occurred to me that the attitudes of *I Love Lucy* in the fifties were simply being regurgitated in the nineties. Sure, what constituted fashionable femininity has changed. Lucy was always modest, pretty and well-groomed, while the girls in *Baywatch* are scantily clad, windswept and active. But sadly, the underlying premise is the same.

And the same is being said of men. The body, the image, the style is more important than substance, than spirituality, than integrated sexuality.

Head off to your local newsagency and read the covers of the most popular magazines. They are about fashion, image, beauty, weight loss, sexual technique, diet and such like. We are constantly being bombarded by television and films and magazines with the message that looking good for the opposite sex is our purpose in life. I believe that this obsession will do more harm to gender relations than the stuffy, Victorian attitudes of the church last century did.

In his book, *A Sneaking Suspicion*, John Dickson quotes from an advertisement he saw for a business seminar on how to dress. It goes like this:

> *Successful people know that you must look good to succeed. . . You always make some kind of statement with the way you dress, powerful or inept. . . People think that the way they dress doesn't really matter. But it really does. The most public thing about you is the way you look. Dress right ---- get what you want. . . Come and find out how you can get whatever you want through your image. . . Dressing To Win ---- in only one afternoon you can change your life. . . It's only $95.[1]*

Even in the business world, we are being told that images of sexuality are more important than a deeply integrated sexuality and spirituality. 'Dress right — get what you want' is one of the most pathetic slogans I've ever heard and it's based on a view that style is more important than substance.

Actually, Dickson quotes from John 10, verse 10, (where Jesus says, 'The thief comes only to steal and kill and destroy; I have come that they may have life and have it to the full') and asks the pertinent question as to whether one of those thieves who have destroyed our lives might be the fashion/beauty industry. It's a valid question to raise.

But it's not just fashion that determines success these days. It's body shape and size. We are victims to a culture that imagines thin is beautiful and very thin is even more beautiful. And we deify thin, beautiful women as models of femininity. And yet even though the so-called supermodels are human freaks, we never question the sense behind it. The average model is 172 centimetres tall (Elle McPherson is, in fact, 180 centimetres tall), while the average Australian woman is 162 centimetres in height. That's a ten centimetre difference. And while the average Australian woman weighs 65 kilograms, the average model is around twenty-five per cent lighter than that.

What's the impact on our view of femininity when women ten centimetres taller and twenty-five per cent lighter than most of us are paraded around on our television screens and in our magazines as being 'perfect'? We now have skinny little nine-year-old girls with the figures of toothpicks complaining about how fat they are!

In a recent survey of 1200 people aged 16 and over by Quantam, an Australian market research company, forty-one per cent of the women interviewed and twenty-eight per cent of the men said they were highly concerned about their physical appearance. And it's not that the rest of us don't care: fifty-six per cent of women and sixty-six per cent of men said they were moderately concerned.

With all this worry about our bodies, it's little wonder the body image industry is booming. In our desperate quest for a beautiful, thin body, eighteen million Australians spend $3 billion a year on cosmetics, toiletries and fragrances, $300 million on dieting, $300 on fitness and $20 million on cosmetic surgery. And let's face it, the lie that says our value is based on our looks is an effective selling tool. It places us in a perpetual state of dissatisfaction. The less content we are, the more we consume.

Masculinity and femininity have now become popularly perceived as expressions of 'sexiness' or raunchiness, not sexuality. And it's dangerous. Psychiatrist Ron Kalucy says:

> The idea of thinness as a source of attraction is extremely deviant historically. Almost all societies up until now have thought that being plump or fat is a sign of good health ---- a sign that you're well looked after, that you've got a good provider and that you're highly fertile. Even Marilyn Monroe, the symbol of all things feminine in the fifties, looks like a 'before' picture in a weight-loss advertisement compared with current so-called 'beauties'.[2]

The harm done to our bodies in this quest for image is matched only by the damage done to our self-esteem. This perverse belief that skinny equals success means that our bodies have become demons, capable of making our lives hell. Food, the sustainer of life, is our worst enemy.

Since feminist writer, Naomi Wolf, wrote her best-selling and groundbreaking book, *The Beauty Myth*, several years ago, these anomalies have been on the public agenda, but nothing much seems to have changed. Wolf claimed that beauty is the last of the old feminine ideologies which still has the power to control women. 'It has grown stronger, to take over the work of social coercion that myths about motherhood, domesticity, chastity and passivity no longer can manage,' she says.[3]

I happen to think this cultural lie called the 'beauty myth' (thanks to Naomi Wolf) affects men as well as women, but I can't help but be swayed by her rage at the injustice such a myth plays on women in particular. Female attractiveness has been tied up with youth, while male appeal has to do with power. It's apparently easier for men to age because men with power are frequently older and that's where a man's attractiveness comes from. In films, it's common to see aging actors like Sean Connery or Anthony Hopkins teamed romantically with actresses young enough to be their daughters, but never the reverse.

It is true, however, that the naked male body is being used to sell products nearly as much as the naked female body. Recently, there were great roars of approval from the feminist lobby when Sheriden sheets erected massive billboard displays of a naked, muscular Adonis lolling engagingly on his bed, his Sheridens strategically placed around him. Since then there has been an avalanche of such naked hunks: the Diet Coke bloke is unmistakable, as is the guy in an ad for Zino ('The Fragrance of Desire').

On a recent visit to Manhattan, I was confronted by the largest billboard I have ever seen, over Times Square. Its subject: a semi-nude rap singer, Marky Mark, about to pull down his Calvin Klein underpants. Louis Nowra pursues this trend to the average bathroom:

> *The desire to look good is everywhere. Male bathroom cabinets have radically changed. Instead of just a razor and a bottle of Old Spice, there are men's perfumes, skin creams, talcs, deodorants and vitamins. The barber has been replaced by the hairdresser. Whereas men used to rush in and out of a department store, they now linger in specialised clothing shops. They indulge their body and are beginning to view it as a clothes rack.*[4]

It seems we have a choice: either to encounter God's seductive grace or believe popular culture's seductive lies. Please don't get me wrong. I'm not suggesting that fitness, fine clothes or fragrances are evil. I am, however, declaring that it's a lie that these things are the essence of beauty or of human sexuality.

✠ The Bible's alternative view of human beauty and value

Whenever the Bible discusses human beauty, which is relatively rarely, it endorses fitness and health as worthy of pursuit. But it does so on a purely functional basis. The New Testament concept was that human bodies are like the dwelling places of God.

In the previous chapter, we looked at the ancient view around during King David's time that the presence of God dwelt with the Ark of the Covenant. Later, Israel was to believe God's presence dwelt in the Temple in Jerusalem. But by the time the Apostle Paul was writing, the new Christian church knew that God was not living on Mount Zion in Jerusalem, but within the heart of every believer. If, wrote Paul, you believe God resides within you, then treat your bodies like a temple, worthy of God's residence.

If you were naive enough to believe that God actually lived in a temple somewhere, you'd work hard to ensure that the building was up to standard for the ruler of the universe. Well, argues Paul in 1 Corinthians 3, verse 16, if you're sophisticated enough to understand that God's presence is within your very body, treat your bodies with the same respect. In other words, don't pollute your bodies with unhealthy food, drink or other substances, by engaging in disgusting practices, or by gluttony and laziness.

It's very good, sound advice. But never once does he, or any other biblical writer, connect health and fitness with beauty or attractiveness. Be healthy, treat yourself well because God's Spirit lives in you, he says. But true beauty? — ah, that's another matter altogether!

Christianity affirms a different perspective. In fact, that's one of Christianity's best-selling points: it offers *perspective*. The New Testament, in accord with the ancient Jewish writers of the Old Testament, clearly states that beauty is a spiritual thing, not a physical thing. It affirms that true beauty comes from such things as peace, gentleness, love, courage and mercy.

I'd like to suggest that the essence of beauty includes all these inner qualities and can be grouped under the one concept. Yep, you guessed it: *grace!*

How does God respond to humankind? With grace. And he is our best model. We need to recognise that those who've encountered grace and are prepared to be gracious to others have the essence of beauty. But you won't find a new fragrance out on the market called 'Grace: the essence of true beauty'.

Grace is an often forgotten quality, but it transforms the ordinary into the exceptional. In 1 Peter 3, verses 3 and 4, it says:

> *Your beauty should not come from outward adornment, such as braided hair and the wearing of gold jewellery and fine clothes. Instead, it should be that of your inner self, the unfading beauty of a gentle and quiet spirit, which is of great worth in God's sight.*

Gentleness, quietness, resolution, calmness, sobriety, peace, love: these are all expressions of human grace. When people act in gracious ways, they are exhibiting a quality God finds to be unfadingly beautiful.

Note that Peter isn't saying, 'Don't wear fine clothes or do your hair.' He's saying, 'Don't ever imagine that your hair or your wardrobe is the sum total of what makes human beings beautiful.' In fact, this piece of advice occurs in the context of a discussion on gender relations where Peter's primary concern is that men and women behave graciously toward each other. The basic, core belief at play here is the Judeo-Christian notion that

God is far less concerned with outward appearances than he is with the inner beauty of a gracious person.

In 1 Samuel 16, we are first introduced to the future King David when he is just a young shepherd boy. The prophet Samuel had been sent by God to the home of a man named Jesse with the mission of anointing one of his sons as God's chosen future ruler of Israel. God did not reveal the name of the son he would choose, but told Samuel to meet each young man and, when the right one appeared, he would reveal his identity to him.

Seven of Jesse's strapping young sons were introduced to the prophet who, it seems, was taken by the strength, good looks and general appearance of all of them. But upon each introduction, Samuel heard God whisper in his ear, 'The Lord has not chosen this one.'

Finally, the baby of the family, young David, was brought in from tending the sheep in the fields and God says proudly, 'Rise and anoint him; he is the one' — and the rest, as they say, is history.

Why retell that ancient story? Because, at the outset, when Samuel is marvelling at the physical beauty of Jesse's first son, Eliab, God in 1 Samuel 16, verse 7 whispers to him:

> Do not consider his appearance nor his height, for I have rejected him. The Lord does not look at the things man looks at. Man looks at the outward appearance, but the Lord looks at the heart.

And this pretty well sets the tone for subsequent Jewish and Christian thinking. God doesn't concern himself with outward appearances. His relationships with human beings are based on his sheer, unstoppable grace towards them. God looks at the heart and, seeing all, still loves us, still chooses us. We are then called to do likewise: to live by grace — that is, to base our lives on encounters with God's grace and to exhibit such grace to others.

And yet this runs contrary to so much of what I've been talking about. We have been won over by the spirit of this age to imagine that people are worthy of our time or our interest if they are beautiful, successful or talented — or some such other 'sexy' quality. Grace isn't sexy. It's without prejudice or bias. Grace is completely undeserved.

And here's another paradox: even though God is prepared to encounter us within our sexuality and to bowl us over with his unrelenting and seductive grace, that grace is never offered on the basis of our 'sexiness' or attractiveness. The dreadful fact is that none of us are very attractive anyway. His grace bypasses the normal avenues that relationships take. It is offered to the undeserving, not the sexy. But God is, nonetheless, prepared for such grace to be accessed in our wholeness, including our sexuality.

Human relationships are often not based on grace, but on bias, selfishness and personal need. We make determinations about a person's worth based on outward appearances, because we have forgotten how to look within.

Keith Gibbons, a professor of psychology at Murdoch University, has said that being beautiful *does* help you succeed in this world. He says:

> *You can even be found not guilty of a crime when you're beautiful. It's called the halo effect. This says that, if you are convinced about one good thing about a person, for example their looks, you simplify your thinking by assuming everything about them is good.*[5]

We make these kinds of choices all the time, whether in jury boxes or not, whenever we favour the beautiful or the powerful for our own ends.

The key, then, is to learn to look within. We're not naturally disposed towards looking at the heart. We're too busy looking at whether someone's lost weight or put on weight, how large their breasts might be or how long their legs are.

Looking at the heart takes oodles of grace. So let's define grace more clearly. I've spoken of grace by inference in the retelling of some very old Bible stories and by sharing one of my own encounters with God's grace, but let's be more clear about it.

✠ A deeper look at the nature of grace

Grace is *that force in this world which provides for human beings the resources, the tools, whereby human beings might become everything they were intended by God to become in the first place.* I say it's a 'force', because I know of no better way to describe it.

Grace is apparent whenever I seek someone else's wholeness, whenever I desire their personal growth. Grace is apparent whenever I seek the best for another person. Grace is apparent whenever I work towards tooling up another person so that they have more of the resources they require to blossom and become the best, most complete person they, in their uniqueness, could possibly become.

Grace is the key to personal growth, maturity and wholeness. It is evident in God's involvement in this world and is the hallmark of those integrated human beings who seek to access other people in the manner that God accesses them.

Grace is the creative agency in human affairs that makes relationships worthwhile and life worth living. It finds its source in God and, in those who've encountered it, is unleashed to be exhibited by God's people. Those human beings who dare to integrate both the major 'movements' of their sexuality and who strive after wholeness are drawn towards the perfect image of wholeness, God himself. And in the quest to discover God more fully, we will naturally be drawn to encounter his life-changing grace.

God, sex and grace are three of the most wonderful realities to be encountered by those people who hunger for wholeness. In answering the question 'How are we to respond to each other?', three factors cannot be overlooked:

*   God provides the model for an integrated humanity. He is the source of all reality and therefore the end of all searching.
*   Sex and human sexuality offer us clues to God's nature and to our own destiny. The two major 'movements' of masculinity and femininity, when integrated, provide the material for under-

standing the paradoxical God we are yearning to encounter.

* Grace is the energy that finally bridges the gulf between ourselves and God and which becomes the glue for meaningful, useful human relationships.

I've mentioned that grace is a force or a power that promotes wholeness, overcomes sin and offers acceptance. But it's more. Grace is also a renewing power. In a sense, grace is everything that God does for humanity in Christ — and that includes what he does through individuals who offer themselves to his service. The word 'grace', then, stands for how God relates to human beings and how we relate to him and to others.

Throughout the ages, great Christian thinkers have offered slightly different perspectives. Augustine saw grace as a force in the inner life of a person, calling them to faith and assisting them to live more completely by overcoming selfishness. Aquinas reckoned that grace was a new form of being: it was a supernatural nature bestowed upon the faithful by God that assists us in living more like God. Martin Luther saw grace as God's promise of mercy and forgiveness in spite of our sin.

The Council of Trent defined grace as forgiveness, too, but much more. Grace is primarily an inner renovation of an individual, giving him/her a new birth into a new form of life. And Karl Rahner quite delightfully called it God's gift of his very self to human persons in love. What, then, is grace? Surely, it's at least all these things.

The bottom line for grace is that it offers *freedom*.

When God, like a grand Cosmic Lover, bestows his favour upon people as we saw in the previous chapter, it sets them free. It sets them free from the dreadful yearning for self-justification and affirmation that most people sense. We no longer require all the trappings of beauty, attractiveness or success, because we recognise our beauty and our worth is based on God's grace toward us. This brings a remarkable sense of liberation. We don't have to *try* so hard any more. We are assured of acceptance and this makes it easier for us to accept ourselves.

So it's not so surprising to recall that the image of freedom dominates the biblical stories about grace. Those of Hosea and Ezekiel are classic examples with their heavily sexual allusions. But freedom is sketched on the bigger canvases of biblical thinking. From the freedom from slavery in the Exodus to the freedom from sin and death in Christ, the idea of what God communicates to human beings by his grace is centred around the theme of freedom.

Alternatively, in contemporary Western culture, the desperate yearning for physical beauty, financial success or prestige belies a terrible insecurity, a desperate desire for acceptance beyond achievement. This is the essence of the freedom offered by an encounter with grace.

Charles Revlon, the cosmetics manufacturer has said: 'In the factory, we manufacture cosmetics. In the store, we sell hopes.' And it's about as pathetic as that, isn't it? I have no objection to cosmetics or fragrances, but when they are worn as expressions of hope — the hope for acceptance and success in love — then we can see how shallow our age has become. To transform this world into a place where we encounter each other graciously, generously and without ulterior motives is the goal of every person who has become committed to God's agenda. As the American writer John Powell says: 'Love rejects the question, "What am I getting out of this?"'

I am convinced that if human beings abandoned themselves to the power of God's grace and modelled themselves on him, working to integrate both sexual 'movements' within themselves, we would become a place where grace and harmony and oneness could reign. As it is, there is war between the sexes, war between all humans, war between God and humans. Grace is the ultimate weapon in global and cosmic disarmament.

The difficulty I have in writing this is that you can't *teach* grace to others. Grace can only be shared in love in the context of a loving friendship. I recognise that this will be difficult for some. I don't believe you can go to a workshop or a seminar and *learn* grace. There are no shortcuts on this one. It takes a lot of time to share grace.

Have you ever wondered why, if Jesus had such great power to heal, he didn't just zap the whole world before he died and make everything and everybody well? Why did he deal with so relatively few people during his lifetime? It's because he was living out a model for us. He didn't just 'zap' the world because he knew he had to love the world and you don't ever love someone by 'zapping' them.

The Edict of Milan in AD 313 is a classic example of enforced grace. The two rulers, Constantine and

Licinius, met in Milan and determined that Europe would be Christian. At first, there were only generous enducements for all to become Christian, but after a while this was translated into severe penalties for those who did not. It's like martyring people for refusing to have faith. It was like 'zapping' everyone into the church. (As an aside, it was the beginning of the dreadful decline into institutionalisation that has dogged the church ever since.)

Well, isn't everything we've said about beauty just an example of the way modern people seek to 'zap' themselves into feeling acceptable or attractive? We are all looking for the quick fixes, the easy options. It's easier to work out, buy clothes, get your hair done and slap on some foundation than it is to truly be free to accept yourself. Such freedom comes only by way of grace.

Quite simply, when someone has learned to love themselves because they have encountered God's grace, they are transformed to love others genuinely. This is a tough one for many people. But I'm convinced that loving yourself is the only means by which we can love others. If I can't love myself, I will be forever looking for affirmation in other people. My relationships and friendships will be based on my nagging need to be affirmed as having worth or value. Therefore, my relationships will not be friendships of grace, but alliances of need.

The only way to be freed to love others is to learn to love yourself. How can I love myself? By finally recognising that God's grace means I am somebody worth loving. In fact, to refuse to love yourself is to be rude to God. When you tell him that you're not lovable, you make him out to be a liar, because he *does* love you!

One of my favourite episodes of *The Simpsons* is where Lisa Simpson falls in love with her substitute teacher, Mr Bergstrom. He is witty, charming, urbane, intelligent, cultured — everything every other man in her life (Homer, Bart, et al) is not! Her life is transformed by this wonderful man and she develops a childhood crush on him. He is, in many respects, the Christ figure in this episode. And he fills her life with meaning, purpose and challenge. She has a new inquisitiveness about life because of Mr Bergstrom.

Well, one day she turns up for school and her regular teacher has returned! She races down to the railway station where Mr Bergstrom is boarding a train to take him to the next school. She throws herself at him and begs him not to leave. How will I survive without you, she wails. You can't go, she cries. All to no avail.

I must leave, he tells her. But before he goes, he takes out a pad and a pen and scrawls a note to her and, as he does, he says: 'Whenever you feel that you are nothing, that your life is unimportant and that there's no reason to go on, remember this.' And he folds the note and passes it to her as the train leaves the station to speed him from her life.

As she watches him disappear into the distance, Lisa unfolds the note and reads it. The camera zooms in on the cartoonish handwritten letter. It says, 'You are Lisa Simpson.'

Mr Bergstrom, the Christ figure, leaves her. But before he goes, he fills her with a sense of her own value and importance, her own meaning and significance. This is grace! And in offering grace to young Lisa, Mr Bergstrom frees her to love others and be gracious to them. Mr Bergstrom isn't just the Christ figure, then. He is Everyman and Everywoman. He, by imitating Jesus, is a model for us.

Grace is the way out of this mess we've got ourselves into. As Albert Schweitzer once said: 'The only way out of today's misery is for people to become worthy of each other's trust.' And the way to earn each other's trust is to live by grace. Live by grace — how sweet the sound. Grace frees us to love others.

In the theology of Thomas Aquinas, grace appears in human will as charity. In other words, when grace as a theological experience of humankind hits the road, it becomes charity. Even for Martin Luther, when an individual encountered God's grace, it was reflected in their love for their neighbour. Luther, a 'big' thinker when it comes to grace, was convinced that we oughtn't to love our neighbour in order to love God, nor that we should love God through loving the neighbour.

Rather, when we encounter grace — that is, an experience of God's seductive love — we are freed from the insecurities that normally inform our relationships so that we are able to love our neighbours for their own sake.

So how are we to respond to others? When we encounter the paradoxical nature of God's love and are seduced or won over by his grace, we are freed from our fears and made able to respond to others in grace. And isn't this what sexuality is all about? Isn't it the energy for connection that drives human beings toward each other? If our sexuality is boiled down to the quest to gratify some animal-like lust, it becomes the energy that divides. It becomes an energy that drives us to use people for our own ends.

But true sexuality — always much more than simple genitality — is the energy of attraction and connection. It's part of the package known as the human condition that brings people together. So is our spirituality. Each of them operate in slightly different ways, but essentially, in human relationships, they bring people together. Therefore, grace is the key concept here.

Grace breaks down barriers. Grace is loyal, merciful, compassionate. Grace is creative and productive. Grace always loves with a tough, unrelenting, uncompromising love similar to God's. Grace is holy. It is an expression of rightness, of purity, of perfection. Without it, we might as well pack up our spiritual box-and-dice and descend to the level of the animals, driven by impulses of desire to eat, procreate, sleep or fly south for the winter. But if we dare to tease out expressions of grace in our own lives, we need to recognise that its true source is with God.

When we have encountered the grace of God, then we are fit to rise above our impulses and become god-like in our relationships ourselves. Becoming more like God is, underneath it all, one of our deepest desires.

We can only get closer, the more we're prepared to admit the impossible nature of the task and to offer ourselves to the mercy of God's grace.

11

SEX AND GRACE

How to make great love

It's just as Christian to get down on your knees for sex as it is for religion.

Larry Flynt

Q: Why won't Baptists have sex standing up?
A: Because it could lead to dancing.

Anonymous

OF COURSE, IT HAD TO HAPPEN. We couldn't avoid talking about sex forever. And why should we? I know I began our discussion on sexuality by bemoaning the fact that everyone wants to talk about how to have sex, but no-one's too interested in discussing sexuality/spirituality issues. But I don't want to imply that we can ever really separate the two. As a sexual being, I happen to be a male. I have certain secondary sexual characteristics that identify me as being a male.

I also behave on the basis of the strong masculine archetype that has been teased out of my unconscious by many years of conditioning. I'm working on teasing out those feminine characteristics that lie dormant within me in the attempt to become more whole, more complete, more God-like and more gracious in my relationships. But it's impossible for me to divorce all that stuff from my very basic desire to have sex. In recognising and championing my sexuality, I can't imagine that the physical craving for sexual pleasure should not ever be considered. So let's consider it!

How does God imagine we should have sex? Yes, *graciously!*

Remember, if we learn to integrate our sexuality, to truly embrace a commitment towards wholeness, that will draw us closer to becoming more like God. He is wholeness. But ultimately, that journey will only take us so far, because we are fundamentally flawed creatures. Wholeness is a great ideal and worth striving for, but we must always bear in mind that, when striving leaves off, God's grace takes over. He loves us, chooses us, nurtures us, seduces us, in spite of our flaws and our poor choices and our betrayal of all our best ideals.

Grace, then, becomes the hallmark of God's relationship with us and the model for our relationships between the sexes (well, in all relationships, really). Loving, nurturing, choosing and protecting are expressions of grace. Even though the one we love might betray us, abandon us or just plain disappoint us, grace demands we press on, continuing to love, nurture, choose and protect. It's what God would do. In fact, it's what God *does* do.

Violence is the most supreme denial of grace. Violence in relationships is the antidote to grace. When one person inflicts physical suffering on another, grace has no foothold. Grace demands we always tease out personal growth. Because violence is destructive, it is the opposite of grace.

In relationships, violence can take several forms. It can be physical and we all know what physical violence looks and feels like. But violence can also be verbal. Abusive language, belittling taunts, unfair criticism are all manifestations of violence. Violence can also be financial. The refusal to share, the oppression of another on the basis of an unfair distribution of resources, is violence. When one partner determines who the other partner can or can't see, or what the other can or can't do, this is a manifestation of violence. Violence need not just be physical. It can be emotional, psychological, social, sexual and spiritual.

The people of grace are sharers, nurturers, carers, stewards of love. They are loyal, merciful and forgiving. But remember that grace is tough. It is always on the side of the right. It will not tolerate inequity. It is fair, just, impartial. Grace is just like God, because grace is one of the best expressions of his holy and loving nature. If we want to be whole, an increasing manifestation of such wholeness will be the ever-deepening expression of grace in our lives.

When we come to discuss what a sexual relationship between two lovers should look like, we must maintain this basic rule or framework in our thinking. *All* relationships should be gracious in nature, *including* sexual relationships.

Sex as discussed in the Bible is always considered very carefully. Underlying all this discussion, the Bible has a basically very positive and optimistic view of human sexuality. But this optimism is overlain with many instructions, rules, regulations, advice and suggestions. So much so, in fact, that casual observers of the biblical view of sexuality have imagined that the Jews and the Christians are down on sex. But not so! We are entering the realm of yet another one of those delightful paradoxes so common in Judeo-Christian thinking.

On the one hand, God says sex is good. On the other, he gives his people all these restrictions on its expression. So which is it? Is sex good or not so good? Why place limitations on something that is supposed to be a perfectly normal expression of human experience?

✠ God elevates the everyday to the level of the holy

For us to truly appreciate the Christian view of sex, we need to understand this paradox. And to begin to embrace this understanding, we must start with the awareness that the Bible does not divide the world into the sacred and the secular. I know the church has done this for centuries, but that has been a fundamental error on its part. In the Bible, *everything* comes from God and is potentially sacred.

The church has always taught that certain things like prayer, meditation, worship, Christian service, biblical teaching are sacred activities, while eating, sleeping, working, making love and playing sports are secular activities. The sacred activities have been God's affair, while the secular activities have been matters that don't directly concern him. They are the affairs of mere mortals.

But at the very outset of this book, I pointed out that I believed eating, sleeping and making love were deeply spiritual activities. It's a mistaken notion to imagine that God sees our need for sleep or food as being a mere trifling, an annoying pastime that inconsequential humans have to be concerned with. In fact, the Bible affirms that, through food and sleep, God has been known to access human beings very significantly.

At the college where I teach, there is a theology lecturer who often makes much of the deeply spiritual experience of watching the Australians play test cricket or a day-night game under lights at the SCG, and he's not fooling. For Ross Clifford, God is very tangibly present in the atmosphere of celebration, camaraderie, eating, drinking, sharing, laughing or mourning. At our weekly college chapel service, he preached a sermon, 'A Theology of Idleness', where he implored our students to see God in the experience of picnics, barbecues and test matches.

In essence, Ross is saying what theologian Martin Buber said years before. Buber pointed out that, while many of us tend to see the world as divided into the realms of the religious (the sacred) and the ordinary or non-religious (the secular), the reality is quite different. He believed that the division should really be between the sacred and the not-yet-sacred. Everything in God's world can be sacred if you realise its potential sacredness.

The mistake that the Christian church made was to forget its Jewish origins. For centuries, Christian mystics were trying to escape the world of the secular into a sacred, religious, holy existence. This meant that they denied their ordinary, non-religious cravings, like food and sex and comfort. It was considered sacred to abandon these things as much as possible.

But the Jews never taught such a thing. In the Old Testament, there is no denial of the so-called secular needs of human beings in preference for more 'holy' pursuits. Rather, as Martin Buber reminds us, the goal of Judaism is not to teach humans how to escape from the profane, non-religious world to the cleansing presence of God, but to teach humans how to bring God into the world, how to take the ordinary and make it holy!

Instead of thinking of ordinary, everyday activities such as eating as mundane and unholy, let's consider how we might see them as an opportunity to bring God and his grace into our everyday world. Well, the Jews did this primarily through a very complex series of dietary laws. Yes, dietary laws! By applying very tight restrictions on what you can and cannot eat, the Jews elevated the simple practice of eating to a sacred level.

Everyone has to eat. Animals have to eat. We all do it every day, if we can. For most of us, eating is so ordinary a thing; we barely give it any deep thought. Sure, we spend hours thinking of what to eat, where to eat or with whom to eat, but we never think more deeply about its potential to become a holy event. By placing 'religious' limitations on diet, Judaism insists we reflect on the holiness of feasting.

Think about it. What the Jewish way of life does by imposing rules on our eating, sleeping or work habits is to take the most common and mundane activities and invest them with deeper meaning. It turns every one of these activities into an occasion for obeying or disobeying God. So if you walk into McDonalds with a Jew and you order a cheeseburger, but he refuses, you are just having lunch, but he is making a theological statement. It's called 'making the ordinary extraordinary'.

The apostle Paul struggled long and hard with this issue. In the very early days of the church, many Jews had converted to Christianity along with many pagan Gentiles. The Jewish Christians were foisting their dietary laws onto the Gentile Christians. They claimed that you couldn't be a good Christian and not eat kosher. Paul eventually came to take the view that God's grace was an expression of his favour towards all people irrespective of their diet. He argued that it didn't really matter what you ate, as long as you did so with an attitude of devotion to God and a clear conscience (he also gave a useful bit of advice on how people should handle their differences of opinion on this matter!).[1]

Paul claimed that grace gave us freedom. And he was right. We no longer have to be worried about whether God will condemn us for eating a cheeseburger. But I don't believe Paul ever intended for us to throw the baby out with the bathwater. In fact, he says, 'Eat anything sold in the meat market without raising issues of conscience, for "The earth is the Lord's and everything in it".'[2]

It's all right to eat anything you like, he says (though he goes on to caution Christians about not causing offense or embarrassment or misunderstanding to your guests or hosts). God's grace frees us from neurotic fears of upsetting him by putting a foot out of line. But how can he say it is okay to eat anything sold in the meat market? Because 'The earth is the Lord's and everything in it'. In other words, you can break the old dietary laws while ever you remember where every blessing comes from.

Sadly, we have broken away from the very useful restrictions of the Jewish dietary laws *and* we've forgotten that every good thing in this world comes from God and can be celebrated as a holy activity. The ancient laws meant that the hours you worked and the food you ate were religious decisions. We Christians, in rejecting the narrowest definition of restriction, have allowed the ordinary to remain ordinary.

I believe we ought to eat like Paul ate, by recognising the importance of raising the mundane to become holy, by being free to eat what we choose, but by choosing to make the ordinary holy. When Paul was offered a pork chop for dinner by a Gentile host, I'm sure he would have eaten it out of respect and gratitude, knowing God would not judge him. But, I speculate, insofar as he had control over his own diet, he would have maintained a commitment to the rigours of his Jewish heritage, not out of fear or habit, but in order to bring his God into the everyday, into the ordinary.

This, I believe, was Christ's concern when he initiated the Lord's Supper. He wanted Christians to see that eating and drinking were legitimately religious activities through which our devotion to Christ could be properly expressed.

I know many people will not be buying this. Some

people have told me that to be a Christian is to abandon the restrictions and limitations of the Law of Moses. And I agree that grace overrides law every time. But can't we live with both? Can't we see the value of a law that elevates the everyday stuff of living into the sacred *and* live in the knowledge that, when we blow it by being unable to fulfil such a law, God still loves us deeply? I believe we can, though I personally don't eat kosher. I do, however, think it's not kosher to be gluttonous or a drunkard. I do believe we ought to eat and drink well and do it as a holy event, and I think restrictions help elevate the ordinary.

A clear expression of this idea can be found in the film, *Babette's Feast*. It's the story of a Parisian woman who, escaping political tyranny in France, finds herself in exile in a tiny, austere Lutheran village in Denmark. There, she merges unobtrusively into the puritanical community, her only tie with France being the lottery ticket sent to her every year by an old friend. After fourteen years of austerity, she wins the 10 000 francs prize money. Rather than escaping her exile after years of enduring plain and soulless food, she decides to blow all her money on a truly French banquet.

It is a triumph of culinary art. Its preparation is almost a religious experience, but sadly only one of her guests recognises it as the masterpiece it is. After fourteen years of self-denial in exile, Babette's feast is a celebration of sacrifice, festivity, fine food and hard work. It is a powerful reminder that the act of savouring must entail a degree of gratitude. Enduring her plain drudgery for so long only serves to heighten Babette's banquet to the realm of the sacred. Her 10 000 franc feast is a holy event only *because* of her years of denial.

It is a basic Judeo-Christian belief that we can only know real freedom or real pleasure through sacrifice and hard work. We tell stories about the Jews escaping the slavery of Egypt into the freedom of the Promised Land after forty years of sacrifice. We celebrate the freedom of eternal life that comes only through the sacrifice of the cross. We know a concert pianist can only know the freedom of playing a concerto by Bach after the sacrifice of many years of playing scales.

In much the same way, Harold Kushner, a rabbi, calls Jewish dietary laws spiritual calisthenics, designed to teach us to control the most basic instincts of our lives. He says:

> We [Jews] are not directed to deny or stifle [our appetites], but to control them, to rule them rather than let them rule us, and to sanctify them by dedicating our living of them to God's purposes. The freedom the Torah offers us is the freedom to say 'no' to appetite.[3]

Kushner's point is that, as it's necessary to live a free, healthy, productive existence, we need to develop the skills to discipline our lives. We need exercise or practice in saying no to our cravings. Again, I need to point out that I'm not advocating a return to every one of the Levitical dietary laws which permit certain meats (cows, sheep, chicken, fish) and forbid others (pigs, shellfish, birds of prey); which determine how, where and by whom animals are to be slaughtered and meat prepared; which forbid the mixing of meat and dairy products at a meal. But let's face it, we should be factoring some kind of restrictions into our habits to equip us for living more sacred lives.

What's this got to do with sex? Everything!

✠ God elevates the sexual experience to the level of the holy

All that I've said regarding food and eating is equally applicable to sexual practice. Our desire for sexual gratification is a human craving similiar to our other appetites. Those people who are committed to wholeness know that restrictions or limitations on sexual conduct are not a major blow to our sex lives, but a way of heightening sexual experience into a sacred event.

Animals eat and procreate on the basis of instinct and desire, without discipline or forethought. As Clark Ellzey says: 'If sex is sought on the animal level, nothing but animal returns can be expected.'[4] Human beings, striving towards the wholeness God calls us to, should know that these instincts can be more than ordinary drives or cravings. They can be sacred acts. They can be elevated to the extraordinary.

I've already looked at how the laws in the Old Testament place great expectations on the consumption of food. Well, they do the same on the practice of sex. And this brings us back to our original paradox. Yes, God says sex is good, but places limits on its expression, not because he really thinks it's bad, but so we can heighten the ordinary event of intercourse to the extraordinary level of the holy.

God thinks food is good. God thinks the fruit of

the vine is good. God thinks deep sleep is good. God thinks hard work is good. But in every case, he puts restrictions on the degree to which we will enjoy them — not to limit our enjoyment, but to encourage us to bring him into these things.

The writer G.K. Chesterton once noted the importance of factoring God into every good thing in our lives. He captured this idea of making so-called secular activities sacred when he said:

> You say grace before meals. All right, but I say grace before the concert and the opera, and grace before the play and pantomine, and grace before I open a book, and grace before sketching, painting, swimming, fencing, boxing, walking, playing, dancing, and grace before I dip the pen in ink.[5]

It's not that God doesn't want us to enjoy perfectly legitimate pastimes like the theatre, the beach, the race track or the sporting field, but he desires us to factor him into these things in significant ways. It's not uncommon for the surfing community to have a heightened sense of God's presence in the sea and surf, but why can't cricketers, painters or gardeners see that playing cricket, painting or gardening are activities for which we should thank God?

When God, for example, insists we give over a day each week to worship him, it's not so that every seventh day he can enjoy our flattery; it's so that we will factor a religious aspect into our work habits. When he insists we not drink to excess and become drunk, it's not that he is a wowser, but because he wants us to bring him into the bar with us.

If I refuse that one more drink just because I fear being breathalised on the way home, it has been a very ordinary evening, hasn't it? But if I drink sensibly because God has called me to do so, I'm drinking with God — an entirely extraordinary concept! Likewise, if I embrace the restrictions he has set for my sex life, I am not sexually hung up. Rather, I am choosing to make the otherwise very ordinary act of sexual intercourse a holy thing.

We shall now look at some teaching from the Bible about sexual relations.

✠ Marriage: the normal, expected life path

In the Bible, there is an implied expectation that the normal course of human existence involves marriage and childbirth. In fact, in the Bible there is no choice enacted in this matter. People didn't *choose* to be married. Rather, they needed to choose *not* to be married. Celibacy or singleness was a choice, not marriage and family life. The normal, expected route for every individual was to be married and to produce and raise children. Any deviation from this route was not frowned upon necessarily. It was simply recognised as not being the norm.

In Judaism to this day, such a view is held. Christianity has had an interesting tussle with this basic biblical mandate. As we've seen on a few occasions, the Christian church went through periods where celibacy was seen as an expression of religious devotion. But I believe this has more to do with remnants of Greek philosophy and Augustinian thought than it has to do with the teaching of the Bible. Sure, Paul goes to great lengths to defend his own choice to become celibate, but he never prescribes such a choice for others. Marriage and parenthood is a good and perfect gift from God and is to be enjoyed by all.

Of course, we need to define 'marriage', don't we? When the Bible speaks of marriage, it is referring exclusively to Jewish marriage. There is no such thing as a Christian marriage in the Bible. In the New Testament, when Jesus attended weddings, they were Jewish. When Paul or Peter speak in their writings about marriage, they have Jewish marriage in mind. The service we know today as the Christian wedding ceremony — 'Dearly beloved, we are gathered here this day. . .' — is a construction by the Christian church. It was made up to express what Christians believed about marriage on the basis of Jesus' teaching and the teaching of the New Testament.

It anticipates that a couple will make a lifelong pledge to remain faithful to each other until they are parted by death. It is done in the presence of God and a gathering of the couple's community of family and friends. It is a high calling and every bride and groom who enter into such a covenant are making pledges, the likes of which human beings rarely make at any other time in their lives. Not even signing a mortgage requires such a commitment.

But basically, that's it. A couple are married when they resolve to be faithful to each other forever, when they make such a resolution before God and when they do it in the presence of several witnesses.

Does the church have to be involved? Well, this is a moot point. Some church leaders would say categorically that, unless the church is involved and a couple's vows are presided over by an ordained member of the clergy, it is *not* a Christian marriage. Others would say that if the couple has made such vows before God and certain witnesses, they are wedded in the sight of God.

Of course, the law of the land has another criterion for marriage. To be legally married, a couple must appear before a registered celebrant (who may or may not be a member of the clergy) and fulfil certain bureaucratic expectations regarding paperwork. That is, of course, unless a couple wishes to register a desire to be in a *de facto* marriage when they file tax returns, buy property, borrow money and so on.

This is certainly not what the Bible has in mind when speaking of marriage. When a couple simply drifts into living together to see if it works out, they are not married as far as the Judeo-Christian definition is concerned. It's not that the Bible is down on people 'living in sin'. It's just that the Bible places so much importance on fidelity, commitment, loyalty, hard work and courage. Any union between two people that is made on a trial basis or without much consideration for the gravity of the decision denies these important values.

A couple must weigh the implications of such a union, consider their options seriously, pray hard, seek wisdom, then make a decision to marry on the foundation of pledges, promises and commitments. Whether you involve the church in that process is your business.

I realise I may be speaking to readers who have

chosen singleness and neither I nor the writers of the Bible decry such a choice. It's just that we need to recognise it for what it is. Singleness is a choice not to enjoy one of the wonderful experiences of human life. Single people might be reading this who have not made the choice to remain single, but have never met the right partner, or have been divorced or separated from a partner by death. Married people might be reading this who are unable to have children.

The Bible attaches no stigma in such cases, but the norm is for a man and a woman to be married in a lifelong union and for children to be born in that union. Just as feasting is a normal experience of human existence, so is marriage. You see, sight is a normal human experience, but some people through birth or misadventure are blind. They are not subnormal. But they cannot experience one of humanity's great blessings. The same principle applies to marriage, which is seen in the Bible as one of the truly rich experiences of life. Bertrand Russell once said, 'Those who have never known the deep intimacy and the intense companionship of happy mutual love have missed the best thing that life has to give.' Marriage is, however, an experience that, through no fault of their own, some people cannot enjoy.

This is not to say that I can't respect a person's choice to remain single on the basis of religious duty. I have several good friends who are Roman Catholic priests. Their choice to be celibate is a decision I must respect and admire. But I cannot see where the Bible implores us to make such a choice. It is an exercise of discipline, but not a biblical requirement.

It reminds me of the joke about the Catholic priest who says to his friend, the rabbi: 'You don't know what you're missing by not eating bacon. Why would God have created something so delicious if he didn't want people to enjoy it? When are you finally going to break down and try some?' To which the rabbi replies, 'At your wedding, Father!'[6]

So marriage and family life is the norm according to the Judeo-Christian teachings and celibacy is a special choice. This leads me on to the second consideration we should make.

✠ Marriage: the only appropriate expression of sexual relations

Sexual relations are only appropriate within the confines of marriage, according to the Bible. I know this has caused many well-meaning people enormous difficulty, but essentially, the Christian view is that sex can be raised to the level of the sacred when expressed within the limitations of a marriage commitment. As with food, the Jews and early Christians sought ways to enjoy sex within limits. They believed that nothing God made was intrinsically good or evil. It depends on what we do with it.

Sex within the confines of the normal practice of marriage is an expression of devotion both to God and to your partner. By joining parts of their bodies, a husband and wife continue their family heritage; they affirm their own individual identities and develop a new, third identity as a couple; and they perpetuate the stream of life. And, of course, they have a jolly good time doing it. In effect, this deep sharing of bodies, histories, families, identities and futures is about an experience of intimacy — a touching of souls.

Since sexuality and spirituality are so closely linked, it stands to reason that the best expressions of sexuality come through partners who are spiritually connected. The deeper the level of relationship, the closer the souls. It's as simple as that. God anticipates sex is best expressed through marriage, because marriage is the best vehicle for two souls growing together over an extended period of time.

I want to go so far as to suggest that this experience of extending and deepening levels of intimacy is a pathway to understanding spiritual realities of ultimate importance. The sexuality-spirituality cycle kicks in better over extended periods. As a couple grows deeper in its levels of intimacy, the capacity for the partners to become spiritually closer — and, therefore, spiritually more alive — naturally increases. And, as this level of spiritual closeness deepens, so does their level of sexual intimacy.

Sexuality can be the conduit for spiritual discovery and vice versa — as long as *grace* is the underlying assumption. Therefore, marriage has a unifying, life-enhancing function.

✠ Sexual relations and procreation
St Augustine's big mistake, and a mistake made by hundreds of Christian writers since him, is that procreation is *the* purpose of sex. Wrong!

Sexual relations as discussed in the Bible are legitimate as a source of pleasure alone. I have suggested this at various points already. That's why it's perfectly acceptable to marry couples who are past the age of childbirth. If the only purpose of sex was for procreation, ministers could be telling every unmarried couple beyond menopause to go to their separate homes and take cold showers. I have married a number of couples in their sixties or seventies, knowing full well the chief purpose of their lovemaking was not to start a family.

This isn't to say that parenthood isn't to be encouraged. It is considered to be a natural consequence of a couple expressing their sexual urges. But the Christian church, after many years of getting it wrong, is recognising the legitimacy of our need for intimacy, for feeling loved and desired, and for experiencing plenty of great orgasms.

✠ Sexual gratification and the single person

Well, I hope all you single readers are still with me. I have simply tried to outline the biblical view on these matters. And, as I've mentioned, the Bible doesn't really place a high value on singleness, only because it was such an unusual choice.

The strongest proponent of singleness in the whole Bible is the apostle Paul — and he was writing of sexual abstinence or celibacy within the context of what he thought was the end of history. It stands to reason that if you think the world as we know it is about to end, there are lots of ways to prepare yourself rather than being worried about who your future partner might be. What, then, has Christianity got to say to single people, whether single by choice or not?

The first consideration is that marriage is definitely not the promised land. I have spoken in terms of Christian ideals so far. We know that just because a couple have married, they are not necessarily either sexual or spiritual superstars. Many single people will know that their singleness often avails them of the time to work on increasingly deeper levels of personal spirituality, while married people have become distracted by sex, setting up homes or raising children (this was one of Paul's primary arguments for singleness).

Many single people will also know that their wedded friends can be miserable in marriage. Somewhere between a quarter and a third of first marriages break up these days. Around the same number of marriages experience some level of violence within the household.

So, even though marriage is the biblically expected norm and that marriage should be the conduit for increasingly deep levels of spiritual and sexual satisfaction, nothing is guaranteed, by any means. If you've ever been to a strongly evangelical Christian wedding and heard the minister or the father-of-the-bride announce at the reception that, because the couple are both evangelical Christians and that God is part of their marriage, everything will surely be rosy, you've probably blanched as I have. Marriage is about hard work and courage. There *are* no short cuts. Grace involves considerable commitment. No so-called 'Christian marriage ceremony' can zap the couple with grace.

If you are single, then, how would God imagine you should express your sexuality? By working on expressing your energy to connect with others; by teasing out your opposite sex gender traits; by seeking to become more like God; by encountering grace and by being gracious. Single people, as Paul says, have the time, the space and the energy to put more into these endeavours.[7]

Everything I've said about sexuality and spirituality ought equally to be applicable to married and single people. If it's the issue of how, according to the biblical restrictions, a single person can express his or her need for genital sexuality, that's another, related question. Paul says, 'Now to the unmarried and the widows I say: It is good for them to stay unmarried, as I am. But if they cannot control themselves, they should marry, for it is better to marry than to burn with passion.'[8] So, it's better to marry than to burn.

But if you do not marry, how do you deal with the burning? The Bible is not too helpful in this regard. As Paul says, if you cannot cope with the apparent frustration of sexual abstinence, then get married! Easy for him to say.

I think the answer lies with *grace*. You're probably not surprised to hear me say that. Not only ought we to treat others with grace, but we must learn to treat ourselves with grace. Single people need to take special note. Single people should treat themselves with the utmost kindness and favour.

Since unmarried people are missing out on a remarkably expansive sexual-spiritual endeavour, they should pamper themselves with other acts of expansive sexual-spiritual experiences. They should travel a lot. They ought to meet and interact with as many people as possible. They ought to try to attend all the spiritual retreats and all the opening nights they possibly can. They should sleep well, eat well and laugh often.

Singleness is often called a gift, because married life is such an ordinary thing. Don't consider your gift a burden or a millstone, but milk it for everything it's worth. Do things married parents can't do. Read great books late at night. See challenging art-house films. Do evening courses. And it's okay to masturbate. It's not as good as intercourse, but it's still nice and it relieves stress.

(As an aside, many Christian leaders have often discouraged masturbation because of the fantasising that's invariably involved. It's not good, they argue, to fill your head with unwholesome images — and I agree. But let's be frank. A large proportion of married people fantasise during intercourse. Why don't church leaders ever talk about this? Are the fantasies of married people more acceptable than the fantasies of singles?)

But it comes back to grace. I think that it's dangerous and grace-less to fantasise about people you know during masturbation. It objectifies that person purely as a device for sexual release. I think the same can be said when you fantasise about Kevin Costner or Elle McPherson. There is no grace involved. But where's the harm in a single person fantasising about a loving, committed, wholesome sexual relationship with an, as yet, unencountered lifelong partner during masturbation? I know this is a tough call, but singleness is meant to be tough. So is marriage. The best things in life usually are.

Treating yourself with grace also includes knowing yourself and forgiving yourself. Sometimes, we don't understand our own motives. Sometimes we get so far out of touch with ourselves and our own feelings that we're uncertain of our actions. To love someone is to *know* them. If you love your garden, you'll know where every plant is, what condition it's in and what care it needs. You'll spot every weed that raises its purient head. Well, grace dictates we should love ourselves like gardens. We should be aware of what care we need and we should know where the 'weeds' are in our lives.

If we're to be truly gracious to ourselves, we ought to get to know and understand ourselves, our feelings, our reactions, our histories. Then we'll be better served to grow up gracefully. In so knowing ourselves, we'll also be better served to *forgive* ourselves when we don't fulfil our own expectations. Single people mustn't fall into the trap of seeing their perfectly healthy desire for sexual gratification as a curse. It isn't one of the 'weeds'. It's one of the flowering plants that requires tending. So be prepared to forgive yourself more fully when you blow it. God does.

✠ The Song of Songs: the Bible's account of romantic, erotic love

Let's talk about having sex 'Bible-style'. The best material we've got to go on is the erotic love poem found in the Old Testament, called *The Song of Songs*. It is an extended liturgical poem that expresses the strong romantic, erotic love between a man and a woman.

On the surface, if taken at face value, that's all the poem is about. There is no mention of God or grace or law or religion. It is, at one level, a very sexy piece of eroticism.

But traditionally, this has not been good enough for Jewish and Christian scholars. Not that they haven't appreciated it as a celebration of human love, but they have wondered why it was collected as part of the holy scriptures in the first place. This has led them to believe it must have another, deeper, metaphorical meaning.

So traditionally, *The Song of Songs* has been viewed as a portrait of the love between God and his people or between Christ and his church. This isn't at all dissimilar to the line taken by Ezekiel, Hosea and Isaiah as we saw in the previous chapter.

But modern scholars have generally agreed that if we *just* take the metaphorical meaning — that God loves us and desires us like a lover does his beloved — we lose much of the literal meaning in the process. After all, this book contains some very explicit references to human sexual love. I'd like to suggest that *The Song of Songs* has three very important things to teach human beings about having sex and that all three things are shadowed by insights into God's relationship with us.[9]

☐ *First,* The Song of Songs *celebrates an equal, mutual sexual relationship*

This is a very different approach to the one taken back in Genesis 1 and 2. It was the great theologian, Karl Barth, who alerted us to the fact that in the creation narratives in Genesis, we hear the voice of the man indicating his desire and pleasure in having a female partner, but we never hear the female speak. It's implied that she is equally happy about the relationship, but she is mute in her pleasure.

Well, in the Song all that changes. Suddenly, in this idealised relationship, everything is as it should be! In chapter 7, verse 10, the woman in the Song says, 'I am my lover's and towards me is his desire.' Barth reckons that, while the story of the creation of Adam and Eve implies an equal relationship between them, this Song confirms it. In spite of the curse of sin and the resulting disharmony between men and women in Genesis 3 ('Your desire will be for your husband and he will rule over you'), the ideal is presented here in this beautiful poem. Romantic sexual relations ideally take place between equals who are mutually committed to each other.

This is a remarkable expression of biblical teaching on human sexuality. In the Song, the couple's admiration of and yearning for each other is both reciprocal and intense. Both the man and the woman speak clearly and explicitly about their desire for the other. Each considers the other unrivalled. Each praises the physical charms of the other in very explicit terms. And they make clear expressions of their desire to make love to the other.

There is no sense of masculine domination at all. In fact, it's the woman's voice that often speaks the loudest and expresses her passion in the most erotic terms. Hers is not an expression of subordination or subjugation. In chapter 2, verse 16, she sighs, 'My lover is mine and I am his' and then again in chapter 6, verse 3, she says, 'I am my lover's and he is mine.' By repeating the phrase in reverse, she affirms the mutuality of the relationship. At various points, she is as eager to initiate sex as to respond to his invitations. What the Bible teaches about having sex is that it ought to happen between equal partners, between two people whose desire nourishes a love that is freely given and returned.

This reminds us of something about God. He desires us, but he refuses to take us unwillingly. He knows that the best loving is a partnership that acknowledges the joy of being possessed by the beloved as well as the need to possess. We will never be equal to God, but his grace puts in our hearts a desire to be intimate and mutual with him.

◻ *Second*, The Song of Songs *highlights the theme of togetherness and separateness*
The orgasmic joy of togetherness is clearly depicted. They praise each other, embrace and arouse each other and they share the intensity of their passion. But the Song also celebrates their separateness. There are many times when the lover or the beloved is mourning the absence of the other. The intensity of their relationship makes times of separation very difficult, even intolerable, but absence defines presence. It makes it more palpable and pleasing, more excruciating and joyous. It also creates space for reflection and personal growth.

This is an important key. Lovers are never only a couple. Sure, they have a life as a couple, but they must never lose their individual identities to their shared identity. Finding the balance between the paradoxical realities of togetherness and separateness is part of the shared lifelong project of marriage. There are times in any couple's life when one side will be stronger than the other. Then it's time to work on the weak end, whether it be separateness or togetherness.

You probably know couples who are joined at the hip, unable to function properly without their partner. This isn't healthy, because it is a denial of personal spiritual growth. Then there are couples who can live quite happily existing in different worlds, rarely seeing or having much to do with each other. Neither is this the biblical model. A balance is necessary. And the lovers in *The Song of Songs* struggle greatly with the balance. They'd probably prefer their lives to simply be one big, long lovemaking session. But *The Song of Songs* affirms that, no matter how difficult it might be, they need periods of separateness from each other.

Again, there's something here for us to learn about God. I think it's very normal for us to experience times of togetherness or separateness from him. Some people become dreadfully concerned when they can't sense God's presence all the time. Some people feel that God is not present in suffering; others feel he is present in suffering, but not in the so-called daily grind.

I think it's a healthy thing that God seems to be absent at times. I also think it's healthy that he is not running around solving all our problems all the time. His apparent absence forces us to grow up and take some personal responsibility for our lives and our choices. Also, his absence makes his presence all the more palpable and enjoyable.

☐ *Third*, The Song of Songs *shows that a good, healthy sexual relationship involves eroticism*
The Song of Songs lays on eroticism in huge dollops, first in chapter 1, verses 2 and 4:

Woman: Let him kiss me with the kisses of his mouth ----
for your love is more delightful than wine. Take me away
with you ---- let us hurry! Let the king bring me into his
chambers.

And second, in chapter 7, verses 7 to 9:

Man: Your stature is like that of the palm, and your breasts
like clusters of fruit. I said, 'I will climb the palm tree; I
will take hold of its fruit.' May your breasts be like the
clusters of the vine, the fragrance of your breath like apples,
and your mouth like the best wine.

This is not tasteless language, crude and porno-
graphic, but it still is sensual, explicit in its description
of each other's bodies. What they desire to perform
with each other leaves very little to the imagination.

My lover thrust his hand
  through the latch opening;
  my heart began to pound for him.
I arose to open for my lover,
  and my hands dripped with myrrh,
  on the handles of the lock.
I opened for my lover. . .

Every possible metaphor is used to describe their
sexual fascination with each other: colours, perfumes,
spices, flowers, fruit, fields, budding vineyards, luxuriant
gardens. It's as if their erotic desire for each other has
opened their senses to the world around them, heightening their appreciation of every sensual delight. Rather
than becoming completely preoccupied with each other,
their love opens their eyes to a renewed vision of God's

creativity and his goodness.

Sexual relations between committed, mutual individuals ought to be wild, erotic and passionate. All the stories you've heard (whether true or not) about Christian missionaries during the Victorian era travelling to the apparently sexually liberated peoples of Africa to 'teach' them 'proper' sexual etiquitte are a blight on the church. The so-called 'missionary position' that celebrates a static, ordered masculine domination of his partner has little to do with the celebration of orgasmic sexplay detailed in *The Song of Songs*.

Further to this, the woman often boasts of her erotic love life to her friends. And they, in turn, praise her beauty and her good fortune at having secured so satisfying a relationship. In many respects, the passion of the couple's love life is a shared thing. It is a cause for celebration and community joy. These days, the love of a man and a woman seems to be so much more private and isolated. Good Christians don't ever talk about their sex life! But in the Bible, these lovers never shut up about it. We ought to encourage lovers to exult, to speak frankly and openly to trusted friends.

We have already noted in the previous chapter the way the Bible uses human sexual love as a mirror of divine love. God transcends sex, but biblical theology dares to use themes of sex and marriage as metaphors for portraying God's relationship with us. God initiates and passionately pursues a loving relationship with us. Our longing to enjoy his sublime presence is eloquently and powerfully expressed by the lips of the woman of the Song.

Having sex, according to the Bible, involves grace. Treating each other mutually, respecting each other's willingness to give and receive love are acts of grace. Behaving like equals takes grace. Enjoying togetherness, but allowing servings of separateness will take grace on the part of each lover. And sexual experimentation, heightening the senses, inviting the erotic will open us to experience the good graces God has built into this world.

Basically, *The Song of Songs* offers us a very important insight. Both grace that forms human partnerships and is the glue of human community (true human love) and the grace that sustains the whole of creation (divine love) is the one gift of God. In fact, it is the most sublime gift of all. A heightened awareness of one should provide a heightened awareness of the other. The unknown poet who wrote the Song (it has erroneously been attributed to King Solomon) offers this profound yet simple advice in chapter 5, verse 1:

Eat, friends, drink!
Drink deeply of love!

And that about sums it up. Drink deeply of love. Both human and divine love, one the mirror of the other, offer us the resources for living healthy, productive, creative lives. To pursue God is a noble cause, as is the pursuit of a wholesome sexuality.

Eat and drink, friends. These things will sustain you heartily!

EPILOGUE

FINALLY, I FEEL THAT I MUST ADDRESS some of the implications of this material for the church. I have quite purposely not written this book for churchgoing people, but I am a Christian minister and I don't see how you can look to the Bible for insights for modern living without there being implications for the Christian church today.

If I am right in looking at gender differences and seeing that God demonstrates both sets of so-called gender traits, and that in order to be more God-like we ought to integrate our sexuality more in order to grow spiritually, the church needs to wake up. Most of the church's leadership today represents one way of thinking. It is white, left-brain, male thinking. Since the turn of the century, the church has been dominated by good old fashioned 'commonsense' as expressed by obsessive-compulsive white men. And on the strength of it, the church has been going down the drain in the Western world for the past fifty years.

In this regard, there are four matters the church

needs to attend to.

First, the church needs to listen to the women in its midst. The church still considers the term 'feminist' to be akin to 'heretic'. If the image of God is whole, expressing both masculine and feminine 'movements', then the church of God's people ought to reflect this. By ignoring the contribution of women, the church is holding up a defaced image of God to the world and saying, 'Come, let us adore him', but in the current form he doesn't look too adorable at all. When the church learns to integrate human sexuality and to represent the perfection of God (in every individual member and the corporate life as a whole), then it will have a mission in this world again.

It is interesting to consider the degree to which many of the male American evangelical theologians, who have dramatically shaped the Protestant church's views on God, were responding to their own distant and aloof fathers. Many of them, including the greats Carl Henry and Edward Carnell, have left clues in their personal writings to their austere, aloof, fundamentalist fathers. Could it be that the distant, absent masculine God they explored in their public writings was a reflection of their personal search for their own fathers? They were men who grew up in an era when fathers were distant, sovereign characters who supposedly knew all and could solve all. Perhaps their own social milieu has informed dramatically on their reading of the Bible, to the exclusion of the idea of a feminine face to God.

Second, we need to take a good, close look at the differing ways that men and women respond to God. If men and women respond to each other and their world differently, then it stands to reason they will approach God in varying ways, also. Some recent research on the psychology of religious conversion seems to indicate that men respond to God in *transactional* terms. They see themselves engaging in a transaction or a deal with God. They see that he has something to offer them and that they might have something to offer him.

Women, however, are more enamoured of the *relational* aspect of the gospel. They are impressed with the possibility of intimacy with God — of a deep, abiding personal relationship with him.

This is not to say women have it right and men don't. Jesus talks about giving up your life to gain the promise of eternity. He talks about being prepared to be the last in order to become first. This is very transactional language. But he also speaks of intimacy with God. Both aspects are validated by Jesus. We need to be more aware of presenting the whole picture, not just the half.

Third, the church needs to break down the walls of enmity and discrimination that are so common in human affairs. Sexuality and spirituality are different expressions of the human energy for connection. People who have encountered God's grace and are unleashing their energy for connection with each other are blind to differences in colour, race, socio-economics, preferences or histories. God's people must be the most connected, gracious of all groups, and their sexual-spiritual energy for making connections should be so intoxicatingly attractive it could transform all peoples.

It used to be said that eleven o'clock Sunday morning was the most segregated hour in America. Today, the churches are still split between black and white, charismatic and non-charismatic, rich and poor. Is it any different in the rest of the developed world? The church, which ought to be the experts on God, sex and grace, should be the first to know and therefore practise that the power of each of these three realities will destroy the relentless forces that drive human beings apart.

Fourth, the church needs to ease up on its thoroughgoing commitment to left-brain logic. If it isn't rational, logical, demonstrable and clear, the church doesn't seem interested in it. Our theology has become about as interesting as reading Bertrand Russell's *Principia Mathematica*, which is a remarkable irony. Late last century and early this century, the church was attacked for not being rational enough. The modernist, atheist philosophers of the day claimed that if you could prove something empirically, it was open to very grave suspicion. So the church seems to have responded by becoming very clinical, very empirical in all its pronouncements.

Well, blow me down if everyone hasn't abandoned that dry, dusty, unimaginative world that has no sense of wonder, mystery or awe. Today, people are fascinated by angels, the supernatural, auras, energies and forces. We are living in a post-modern world, where right-brainers have a genuine contribution to make. Artists, musicians, novelists and playwrights have a genuine voice today along with mathematicians, scientists and medical researchers. Sadly, the church hasn't caught up.

Our preaching sounds like readings from technical manuals. Our pronouncements lack genuine soul.

The church needs to be a community of imagination and intuition. There are too many people in churches who are great at thinking logically through a theological issue, but can't pray, meditate or reflect deeply. We have to support Christian authors, singers, songwriters, playwrights. Not that I'm suggesting this ought to happen to the exclusion of left-brain logic. It's all about balance and harmony. Essentially, it's about wholeness. The church is dangerously skewed in one direction only.

Fifth (and arising from this), the church desperately needs to rediscover paradox. Sure, right-brainers cope with paradox a lot easier than others, but the church's emphasis on propositional, logically sequential truth won't impress many modern thinkers.

As I have sought to demonstrate, Christian theology is a mass of paradox. We need to come clean and encourage our membership to do a little bit more work themselves. For too long the leadership of the church has packaged their message into logical, bite-sized pieces for congregants. They've made it simple and digestible. But a paradox is difficult to maintain and takes commitment and resolution.

It's time churchgoers were responsible for embracing Christian truth more fully for themselves.

ENDNOTES

Introduction

1. Robert Frost, *Robert Frost's Poems*, Washington Square Press, 1968, p.94
2. *Ibid*
3. Garrison Keillor, *The Book of Guys*, Viking Press, 1993, p.11
4. *Ibid*
5. Keillor, *op.cit.* p.12
6. *Ibid*, p.20
7. *Ibid*, p.21

Chapter 1

1. C.S. Lewis, in Alister McGrath, *A Cloud of Witnesses*, IVP, 1990, p.127
2. Richard Holloway, *Anger, Sex, Doubt and Death*, SPCK, 1992, pp.34-35
3. Simone Weil, in Alister McGrath, *Bridge Building*, IVP, 1992, p.56
4. Lewis, in Alister McGrath, *Bridge Building*, p.57
5. Psalm 42, verse 1
6. Augustine of Hippo, *Confessions*, Sheed and Ward, 1942
7. Augustine of Hippo, *Confessions*, Sheed and Ward, Book 1, p.3
8. Emil Brunner, *The Christian Doctrine of Creation and Redemption*, Lutterworth, 1964, p.63
9. Joan H. Timmerman, *Sexuality and Spirituality*, Crossroad, 1992, p.9
10. James B.Nelson, 'Between Two Gardens: Reflections on Sexuality and Spirituality', in *Studies in Formative Spirituality*, Vol.2, 1981, p.92
11. Sam Keen, *Hymns to an Unknown God*, Bantam, 1994, p.156

Chapter 2

1. Stu Weber, *Tender Warrior,* Multnomah, 1993, p.114
2. Gary Smalley, in Weber, *ibid*
3. Carol Gilligan, *In A Different Voice*, Harvard University Press, 1982
4. Caris Davis, 'Why Do Men Know It All?', *New Woman*, September 1994, p.86
5. Louis Nowra, 'What Maketh The Man?', *New Woman*, September 1994, p.70
6. *Ibid*, p.72
7. Tim Winton, 'The Masculine Mystique', *Good Weekend*, August 27, 1994, p.67
8. Nowra, *op.cit.*, p.72
9. Robert Pool, *The New Sexual Revolution*, Hodder and Stoughton, 1994, p.262

Chapter 3

1. M. Scott Peck, *Further Along The Road Less Travelled*, Simon and Schuster, 1993, p.221
2. Sylvia Chavez-Garcia and Daniel A.Helminiak, 'Sexuality and Spirituality: Friends Not Foes', *Journal of Pastoral Care*, Vol. 39, No.2, 1985, p.161
3. Sylvia Chavez-Garcia and Daniel A. Helminiak, *op.cit.*, p.162
4. M. Scott Peck, *op.cit.*, p.225
5. Mary Hayter, *The New Eve In Christ*, SPCK, 1987, p.41

Chapter 4

1. Soren Kierkegaard, in John Naisbitt, *Global Paradox*, Allen & Unwin, 1994, p.12
2. John Bradshaw, *Creating Love*, Bantam, 1992
3. Robert Bly, *Iron John*, Element, 1990, pp.x-xi
4. Jeremiah 23, verse 23
5. Karl Rahner, *Foundations of the Christian Faith: An Introduction to the Idea of Christianity*, Darton, Longman and Todd, 1978, p.137

Chapter 5

1. Joel S. Goldsmith, *Living By Grace: The Path to Inner Enfoldment*, Harper Collins, 1992, p.71
2. James Montgomery Boice, *The Sovereign God*, IVP, 1978
3. *Ibid*, p.164
4. *Ibid*, p.165

Chapter 6
1. M. Scott Peck, *The Road Less Travelled*, Simon and Schuster, 1978, p.84
2. *Ibid*, p.84
3. Martin Luther King, *Strength to Love*, Hodder and Stoughton, 1963, p.141

Chapter 7
1. Frederick Buechner, *Whistling in the Dark*, Harper, 1993, p.86
2. Paul D.Hanson, in the *Ecumenical Review*, October 1975, p.318
3. George Adam Smith, in W.A.Visser't Hooft, *The Fatherhood of God in an Age of Emancipation*, World Council of Churches, 1982, p.129

Chapter 8
1. Gustaf Aulen, *Christus Victor*, SPCK, 1931, p.103
2. Martin Luther, in Aulen, *op.cit.*, p.104
3. Luther, in Aulen, *op.cit.*, p.105
4. Patricia Wilson-Kastner, *Faith, Feminism and the Christ*, Fortress, 1983, p.90
5. Dorothy Sayers, in Helen Cecilia Swift and Margaret N.Telscher, *Unveiling the Feminine Face of the Church*, St Anthony Messenger Press, 1989, p.32
6. Patricia Wilson-Kastner, *op.cit.*, p.72

Chapter 9
1. Cat Stevens, 'Can't Keep It In', from the album, *Catch Bull at Four*, Island Records, 1972

Chapter 10
1. John Dickson, *A Sneaking Suspicion*, St Matthias Press, 1992, pp.23-24
2. Ron Kalucy, in 'Beauty Can Be Fatal', *West Magazine*, August 6, 1994, p.16
3. Naomi Wolf, in 'Who's Pulling The Strings of Our Lives?', *West Magazine*, August 6, 1994, p.20
4. Louis Nowra, 'Meat Marketing', *Sydney Morning Herald*, October 3, 1994, p.11
5. Keith Gibbons, 'The Thin End of the Wedge', *West Magazine*, August 6, 1994, p.13

Chapter 11

1. See especially 1 Corinthians 10, verses 23 to 11, verse 1
2. 1 Corinthians 10, verse 25
3. Harold Kushner, *To Life: A Celebration of Jewish Being and Thinking*, Little, Brown and Co., 1993, pp.51-52
4. Clark Ellzey, *How to Keep Romance in Your Marriage*, Association Press, 1951, p.171
5. G.K. Chesterton, in Martin Wroe, *God: What The Critics Say*, Spire, 1992
6. Kushner, *op.cit.*, p.55
7. See all of 1 Corinthians 7, but especially verses 32 and 33
8. 1 Corinthians 7, verses 8 and 9
9. For these three ideas, I am indebted to Roland Murphy's excellent commentary, *Song of Songs*, in the *Hermeneia* series, Fortress, 1990.